BrandFix

A Brand Strategy Guide for Busy Entrepreneurs

Kady Sandel

Table of Contents

1. The Basics of Branding: What Branding Is and Why It's Important..................5
2. Naming a Brand..................17
3. Brand Strategy: What's Included in a Brand Strategy and Why You Need One..................27
4. Brand Goals & Objectives..................41
5. Target Profiles..................53
6. Brand Positioning..................63
7. Brand Attributes & Voice..................75
8. Content Strategy..................85
9. Choosing the Right Branding for Your Business..................97
10. Visual Branding..................107
11. Brand Boards and Guidelines..................115
12. Psychology as Universal Communication..................123
13. Designs for Your Business..................131
14. How to Translate Strategy into Visuals..................137
15. Strategic Elements and Execution..................143
    Bonus: Branding Checklist..................149

Copyright © 2019 Ksenija Dulinac, aka Kady Sandel.
All rights reserved.

Front cover design by Kady Sandel @ Aventive Studio.
Interior book design by Bojan Kosic.
Edited by Kelsey Horton, Jackie Dana and Monica Dennis.

1 The Basics of Branding: What Branding Is and Why It's Important

Before I started to write *BrandFix*, I sent out a short questionnaire to people I believed would benefit from knowing more about how to brand or rebrand their business. They were entrepreneurs, freelance business owners, or solopreneurs, and they all had their businesses or side hustles for between six months and three years. All the respondents thought that they already had an understanding of branding; they already had business plans and were making some sales; and all had goals to scale their businesses.

One of the questions I asked them was: "What does 'branding' mean to you?"

By asking this question, I wanted to understand what kinds of misconceptions they might have so that I could help them create an outstanding branding plan to grow their businesses.

Here were some of the answers I received.

Branding to me is:

- Identifying your business by way of visual and brand messaging.
- The visual/physical manifestation of a brand.
- Creating a name for yourself based on how you wish to be perceived.
- The "feel" or experience you leave with your customer/leads.
- A logo design, business cards, website—the visuals.
- The process of creating/storytelling the "personality" of a company.

The fact is that none of these definitions are correct. Branding is not a logo. Branding is not a brand message. Branding is not just the visuals. Branding is not a promotion. Branding is not the "feel" or experience.

If branding isn't any of those things, what is it? Guess what. While it's not any one of those things, it's actually all of them!

Branding is the combination of all the ways you communicate with your clients and your target audience. It's the process of displaying your business to the public through your content and visual identity. All the things that go into building your business presence create your branding, including designing a logo, developing a website with a list of your services or products, spreading the word on all your social media accounts, creating ads, flyers, or videos, going for networking events, and doing email marketing. All of these things go together to form a single picture of your brand identity.

Branding is simply communication. It's what and how your business breathes. It's your company's personality.

As an example, let's consider Apple. What do we know about Apple's branding? The most impactful piece of the Apple brand is their logo—the face of their company. Then, besides the products Apple invents (iPhones, Macs, etc.), they are known for their minimalistic designs, their simplicity, and their store designs. And we all know who Steve Jobs was. Every piece of their branding and public image tics together.

Now, **a brand is not branding**. Someone just asked me what the difference was the other day, so I thought before we go deeper into branding your business, I should explain the difference.

"Brand" is a noun. It's an object. "Branding" is a verb. It's an action. It's what we do with that thing. It's how you communicate your brand to your clients effectively. **Branding is creating a brand.**

Besides those two terms, I know that "branding," "marketing," and "advertising" can sound similar as well. They are all related to each other but are completely different from each other. Those are all tools to help you promote your business. So how are they different?

Marketing is actively promoting a service or product. It's promotion, the process of developing, selling, and providing a product or service to your target.

Advertising is a part of marketing and it's done through ads, which put your product or service in front of potential customers. It's when you pay to have announcements

7

sent to the public and when you try to convince them to buy what you are offering. It's Google ads, Facebook ads, ads in newsletters, and so on.

In summary:

- A brand is an object.
- Branding is the process of creating a brand.
- Marketing is promotion.
- Advertising is typically paid ads/promotion.

You can think of it this way:

Coca-Cola is a brand. When you think about the brand, you think about the red color, Santa, Coca-Cola's truck, family around a Christmas tree. That's branding (everything that makes Coca-Cola). Their Facebook and Instagram stories, videos, and emails are Coca-Cola's marketing. And Coca-Cola's commercial during a popular TV show is paid advertising.

Branding is essential because it's how people will recognize your company. Branding attracts a company's potential clients, it increases brand awareness, and it can set a company apart from competitors. Therefore, it should be memorable because in the end, branding drives new business, makes sales, and increases revenue. And that's what a business is about.

In this book, I will walk you through the branding process in a way that cuts right to the heart of branding for busy entrepreneurs. Let's get started with the most important concept in the book: your brand strategy.

Branding starts with a brand strategy, which is a long-term plan for how your brand will look and feel. A brand strategy is not quite a business plan, but the two are very similar. In both documents, you define who your target is, but in a brand strategy document, you will focus more on how to communicate with that target. Your brand strategy will use all the things that are in your business plan, expand on them, and build a brand people will see, recognize, and remember.

It might be confusing at first, but as we go through the book, these concepts will be easy to follow. In the next few chapters, you will put some of these concepts together to create a brand strategy for your own business. We'll go step by step, as I explain all the terminology and describe real-life examples. (I'll share my branding failures too.) And most importantly: you will learn how to apply these principles to your business and how you can use branding to scale your business.

Branding is challenging, interesting, and definitely powerful. **You can make customers think or feel whatever you want about your brand.** You just need to have your own clear picture about your business, what you offer, whom you offer it to, and how to offer it. You can always improve and tweak your branding as your company and audience grows.

If you've been in business for a while, don't be afraid of rebranding either. It's never too late to start fresh and improve in your customers' eyes.

Before you start creating your own brand, you need to understand branding terminology, define your reasons for creating a brand, figure out the essential branding components, and decide how you will communicate with your ideal clients.

Think about the ways you want your business to communicate with your target market. If your brand were a person, how would it behave? What would its personality look like? Whom would your business need to speak to (your ideal customer), and how would its behavior need to vary to appeal to that person?

When I first started out as a designer, I offered logo designs with no strategy behind them—nice looking marks that didn't speak to the right target, icons that looked great but were on the same level as all stock, not-customized logo designs. Meanwhile, I was so frustrated by hearing from people that my work was too expensive. I was not expensive at all! My work was still okay, but my presentation and my own brand were weak. It looked cheap. I could prove the quality after someone had been working with me, but potential customers were not going to hire me if they were not sure if I could deliver what they were asking for. They needed to know if their logo would work for their brand, they needed to know who my previous clients were, they wanted to see examples, and they wanted to make sure they were investing in their business with the right person.

Also, I had an amazing photo of a cute cat as the main photo of my website. While it's true that I really like cats, that photo made no sense in relationship to my potential clientele and the logo design services I offered.

Looking back, it's easy for me to see why my business wasn't growing. Although I understood design, I didn't yet understand the basics and importance of branding.

When people come across your website, content, and printed materials, do they immediately get a sense of your company's values and voice? Think about how you want your business to sound to others. What do you want them to think about you? How do you want them to feel? Did you notice how many times I said the word "them"? Consider what your brand stands for—and for **whom**. We will be covering these topics and answering these questions for your business later in the book, but I wanted to bring them up now to get you in the habit of thinking from the perspective of your target market.

Here are a couple of companies that have amazing branding: Apple and Nike.

When you go to an Apple store to purchase a laptop, you probably wouldn't research whether the company is high quality (like you would for some other brands), and you wouldn't ask all your friends what they think about Apple. You might inquire about the laptop specifics, size, price, and so on, but you wouldn't ask, "What do you think about Apple in general? Is that a good company to buy a laptop from?" because you already know these answers.

The same with Nike. Usually brand names and logo designs attract consumers to a brand, but at this point, Nike is already an iconic household name. Since you're already familiar with Nike, the logo and visuals are no longer the key factors that attract you to the brand. Instead, you're drawn in by Nike's status and what you know about the company. You've seen Nike ads, all your friends wear "the swoosh," you know they provide quality products, or you're impressed by the clean and well-designed stores. These factors add up to make the Nike brand memorable and consistent.

Both Nike and Apple have mastered the art of making you feel a specific way when you think about their brands.

11

Good branding helps your business by making a memorable impression on customers. If they see your brand, even use your brand, but don't remember it well, they won't come back. Not to mention that they definitely wouldn't recommend it to someone they know. Good branding should tell them what to expect from you before they even buy your product or services. It needs to stand out against competitors and clarify your offer to a potential buyer, showing them that they can trust you. Your branding needs to establish a business and make it easier for people to *remember, recognize, and recommend* you.

A few years ago, I worked with a client who sold amazing skin care products, but her company was dying. She was not making money and her business was falling apart. She couldn't make sales, even though all of her products were outstanding, luxurious, and top-quality.

When she sent me photos of her products, I couldn't believe she was making any profit at all. My first thoughts were: "I'm not sure I would use this even if I got it for free." Literally. Not just from my professional design perspective, but I just felt I didn't trust that product. Besides that, I didn't have any previous experience with the brand – nor had anyone in my circle – and I had never heard the name before. I was not attracted by what I saw, and didn't feel connected, so I wouldn't use it.

So where did she go wrong? Her logo, as the face of the brand, had so many details that you couldn't read it clearly. The typography on her labels also didn't fit the quality of her products. The fonts were serif, italic, and thin, which gave the impression of a weak product that was trying too hard to be different. Her brand colors were light green, brown, yellow, white, and black, and this was just too many colors. The pastel tones felt light and fragile—two words that didn't fit her products or impress her potential customers.

Even though her products were incredible, she couldn't make sales for the price she wanted. More importantly, she couldn't make sales for the prices the products were worth. She simply couldn't prove the quality of her products to potential buyers.

Does that sound familiar? You know your business has potential, but your branding isn't doing it justice?

Before even starting to work on your visual presentation, you need to work on developing your brand strategy. In this particular case, yes, she had a great product with a bad logo, labels, and packaging, but before redesigning all of that, we needed to know who her users were, what we wanted those people to think about the product, and what we wanted them to feel *before purchasing the product*. We needed to determine how to make potential customers excited and trust a product they had never tried before. Finally, we had to decide what we wanted customers to think and feel *after they tried the product*.

Once we had all the notes from the brand strategy document down, we came up with a new logo: a combination mark (a logo that includes symbol and text, such as Lacoste's symbol of crocodile plus the word Lacoste). It was a gradient of bright to dark purple that suggested "shiny" and indicated luxury. We chose sans serif fonts—bold and strong. The logo overall was crisp, contemporary, and timeless, which spoke to her target audience.

Conclusion: **The visual part of branding needs to align with the quality.** Once we rebranded her company, people started to like, buy, and trust it. Her company grew immediately.

Now, think about your brand and consider your offerings as a consumer would. Does it convey value? Does it indicate the level of quality that customers would expect, or does it look cheap? Or does its look suggest it's more expensive than it is?

Most entrepreneurs have businesses that don't send the right messages through their branding, and they don't even realize that's what's costing them business. You can have the best services in the world, but you'll lose business if there's a competitor whose branding is more attractive to your target audience.

Let's do a quick exercise.

What's important to you when you are making a decision about what to purchase? When you see a no-name body wash without a logo next to a body wash with the Nivea logo, which one would you buy?

Most people would choose the Nivea body wash because they recognize the brand.

How would that work if you see two products that appear to be the same but have different packaging and pricing? For example, imagine you see one window cleaning spray that has no logo, its brand name is just text, and the label simply says, "the best window cleaner." Then you see another cleaning spray brand with an attractive logo and a catchy tagline, and it includes a detailed explanation of how to use it. You would probably trust the second bottle, even if its price was slightly higher, because you would feel a deeper sense of trust with that product.

It's the same with what you have to offer. People care how they feel while spending money. Your brand needs to make them feel important, satisfied, and smart. They need to know they are investing their money on something that has good value. Help them make an investment and feel good about it!

Is that something your brand does today? Is your brand that strong? Do people always trust you? Let's see how you can create a brand that people will remember.

2 Naming a Brand

Naming a brand is hard. Renaming a brand is harder.

It doesn't matter if you have a current business or just an idea for one, this chapter will help you understand how people choose names for their brands and whether your name is the right one for your business. We'll explore important concepts regarding your existing name and the meanings of your competitors' names, allowing you to think critically about your brand's name. If you don't have a name for your brand yet, you'll have the tools for how to choose one. On the other hand, if you know 100% that you already have the right name for your business, feel free to skip this chapter or just skim through it.

While it's possible to rebrand and completely redo all of your materials, it's not easy, so it's best to do it right the first time.

17

However, if you realize your brand's name doesn't do you any favors, better change it now than later. Some of the biggest and well-known companies needed to rebrand in order to grow. In this chapter, we will go through real-life examples, and by the end of the chapter you will know what you need to do with the name of your business.

Do you know how long it takes for a company to invent a name? While you can come up with a name for your brand in five minutes and use it, that name may not be something that works well for your audience. Is it something that connects your brand with its consumers? Is it memorable, easy to spell and pronounce? We might come up with a name that we like, but does that mean it's a quality name?

Choosing a good brand name requires more than just creativity, especially if you are doing this for the first time. It's a process and it's up to you (or a person/company you hire) to be different, innovative, and knowledgeable. There are more than 25 million businesses in the US alone. By law, you can't use a name that is already registered and exists — imagine two Amazons or two Apples. It just won't work.

A great name can position you as a true leader in the industry, build brand awareness, and help people remember and recommend your product or service. A clever name is the basic differentiator and separator for your brand. Many of your potential customers might not know anything about your company and a brilliant name can make a great first impression and an instant connection.

It is amazing how important a name can be. It helps a brand's growth and perception. It's the first thing a potential customer hears and sees. Making a powerful impact is one of the main steps in setting up your business for success and branding it. Think about when you last met someone new and imagine your first impressions about that person—his name, his profession, and his voice. What did all of that make you think about him? When it comes to your business and your brand, you need to think about the same things, in the same order.

Brand naming is a systematic process that involves coming up with words and testing different names. It does take time, research, and at least a few people to help you with it. It can be a blogger, a professional naming company, or your brother, but you shouldn't do it alone. You also need feedback from your target audience.

There is a lot of flexibility in inventing a name since it could be anything from your first and last name (or your initials), attributes, services you offer, or words that don't even exist. But how do you know what to do? As mentioned, even if you do have a name already, you should check if it's the right one. If it's not, change it now. Your brand doesn't benefit from keeping it.

Do you know what you want to accomplish with your company? You need a plan with one question in mind: Where do you see your company in five years? You don't need to know the details, such as how many employees you want to have or what their tasks would be, or how many locations you might have. To start with, you just need the basics. Are you planning on being a solopreneur, a business owner with employees, an entrepreneur with multiple business segmentations, or do you want to go international? There are a lot of questions you need to ask yourself, but this should be the very first one.

Whether you're planning on being solo or a company with employees will determine what kind of name you need. There is no best answer here—it's just a question of what's best for your business. If you don't take this into account, your name might end up being too broad or too focused.

You need a catchy and unique name that will help customers remember you. Below you can find some of the techniques I used for my business and that I use for my clients' businesses. There are a few different types of brand names and a lot of options to choose from. This can be a fun and easy process, but it definitely takes time.

Descriptive Brand Names

Your brand name can be *descriptive*, which means it includes a description of what you offer in your name. For example, Burger King sells burgers. This can be great in positioning yourself or your business, but it can also be very limiting. What if one day you want to grow your company and add new offerings, but your name has only that one focus? Of course, Burger King sells fries and soda and other things, but their focus is clearly on burgers. Descriptive names can be effective in terms of recognition, but don't forget to also consider your bigger vision and goals.

Dunkin' used to be Dunkin' Donuts. After they added sandwiches, croissants, coffee, and other items, they realized that their original name was limiting them from growing their brand. This example of rebranding a company name seems easy because they "just" lost one word. But can you imagine how much money they spent on changing all their materials? Yes, it's a big company and they have funds, but they needed to replace all their billboards, store signs, menus, advertisements, branded cups and mugs, and business cards for all their employees—everything that had their logo on it. The moral of the story is to avoid names that are too limiting, unless you know that your long-term goal is to offer only that one thing. For this same reason, I also recommend that you don't use your location in your brand name—you might move or scale your business to other locations. Anything is possible.

I understand the hassle and expense of renaming a company because I have done it myself. When I first started my branding company, I chose the name KD Branding. It had that descriptive word "branding," and it had my initials. It was fine, but once I grew the company, I realized I needed to change it in order to attract my new target audience. KD sounded like a person's name, not like a big company, which was not the image I wanted to keep when I decided to scale my business. Also, every time I would say "KD" they would try to find my website as Kady Branding, and that's not correct. Having "branding" in the name sounded like I was trying too hard to stand out by saying what I do in the name of my business. I was ready to expand beyond the realm of my initials and create a new name that resonated better with my customers. Don't be afraid of rebranding if a fresh new brand will position your company for future success.

Inventive Brand Names

Once I realized that KD Branding was too limiting, I changed the name of my company to Aventive Studio. This was completely different from my previous name, but my company vision and my target were completely different too. Aventive doesn't mean anything. It's a made-up word. It starts with the letter A like a lot of big companies, meaning it will be at the top of alphabetical listings (close to Apple and Amazon!). The letter A is known for being a "leading" letter in human's minds. Don't ask me why, but that's a fact. Aventive also includes the last four letters in 'creaTIVE', 'invenTIVE,' and 'innovaTIVE,' reinforcing the idea that my company is about the ability to create and design something new, creative, and different.

Other inventive company names that come to mind include Sony, Kodak, and Google. These made-up names are very powerful because they don't have anything that limits them. All these companies have a history of why and how they got their name (just like Aventive), but at its core, words like Sony and Google are brand new words. They can be anything and everything.

It is a little bit harder to position an invented name if you're just starting out, but with the right brand strategy it is possible, and sometimes an invented name can make your brand even stronger because you don't need to explain what you offer in your name—you already sound big and independent. A fun exercise that can help is to analyze the names of your competitors and try to figure out why they chose their brand names. We will work on brand positioning in a subsequent chapter, including how to find your true competitors, but I'm sure you already know a few. Do you know why and how your competitors got their names?

How to Create Your Brand Name

When I first started freelancing, I wanted to have my own website with my portfolio because nobody would hire me as a visual designer without one. I didn't know if I should go just by my name as a freelancer or actually create a name for my company even though I hadn't technically created a company yet. (As you can tell—this was all way before I realized that business plans and brand strategy were important!)

My initial list looked something like this: Zebra Designs (because I always wear black and white), White Whiskers (because I like cats), Graphics by Kady, etc. None of it related to my clients, nothing related to design and branding, and these ideas didn't sound special or memorable. And, actually, I wasn't even the one who was making the list. My husband was bored and at home, just putting his ideas down. How professional is that?

As you come up with a name for your brand, you can learn from my mistakes. Even if you don't have a business yet—even if you have a hobby that you are hoping to grow into a business, or just the vague beginnings of an idea for a company—set up your name with your five-year company goals in mind.

When thinking about names and doing research, focus on two main things: **what you offer** and **who your potential customers are.** Do not think about what you like—you are not creating a business name to attract yourself. I see a lot of people making that mistake by saying, "But I really like this, and that name describes me" when the real question is: Does your brand name describe what your potential clients are looking for?

You need to consider whether or not people will be able to remember the name of your business. Sometimes we might think a name is catchy or easy to remember because we came up with it, but that isn't necessarily true. The best way to test your brand name ideas is to share them with other people and observe the reactions they have to your name ideas.

Tell your friends, family, and whomever else you meet that you are thinking about naming your brand and share your name idea with them. Don't explain where the name idea came from or what it means, and don't try to make them remember it. Even if they ask why and how you came up with the name, you can just give a vague answer for now like, "I don't know exactly. I don't remember. I Googled some stuff and this came to my mind."

Then, after a week, ask them, "Hey, do you remember that business name I told you the other day?" Most of them will not remember and that's fine, but if nobody remembers your name idea at all, that's a clear indication that it was not a memorable name. **While this method is not always 100% accurate, it can help you get an idea.** Another cool benefit of this exercise is you will get questions that will make you think, "Why that name?" or "Does it really remind them about a particular service?"

This also depends on if the name is easy to pronounce and spell. Some businesses make a "mistake" in their names on purpose, or try to be clever with spelling, but in the end, you want your customers to be able to pronounce, write, find, and remember your name. So try not to get too creative with adding and subtracting letters to come up with your name.

Name Your Brand!

If you don't yet have a name for your company, or if you're thinking about creating a new name, here's a fun and simple exercise to generate ideas for your brand name.

First: it's brainstorming time. Write down every single possible brand name idea that comes to mind—even if it's just a snippet of a name idea, put it on the list and we will sort it out later.

When you think you're out of ideas, keep going. Add words that describe the service you provide, the name of your street, your dog's name, your favorite color, words from any other languages that you know, your nickname, a river in your hometown... just write it all down for now and gather all the ideas you have. We will worry about whether it fits your business or customers in a minute.

When you think you have a long enough list, pause and look at what you wrote. Now try to branch out from each of those names by coming up with even *more* names that are similar to them. (I told you this list would be long!)

Once your list is longer than you ever thought possible, read it aloud. Remove any name ideas that don't sound right, that are hard to pronounce, or that don't mean much when said aloud. Next, imagine the remaining names printed on your website, business cards, and signs. If any of these names are too long, or if they wouldn't look good on your materials, remove them from the list.

Now think about the names of your competitors and compare each remaining name on your list with your competition. (If you don't know your competitors, refer to Chapter 6: Brand Positioning where we will identify them.) Do your competitors' names sound better than yours? Are their names simpler, more memorable, or just *better*? Remove the names on your list that don't stack up to your competitors.

In the next phase of this exercise, test out the names that are left on your list. Do a quick Google search to see what comes up. Remove any words and names on your list that already exist or are too similar to well-established brands. Besides checking through a Google search, check social media channels as well to see if anyone is using these names there.

Next, test your remaining names by searching for them in Google Images. See if there are any logos, business cards, or flyers with that same name.

Now that you have some name ideas that no one else is using, test them out with your audience. Bounce your name ideas off of your friends, family, and even your current clients to see what they feel is most memorable and remarkable.

Lastly, perform a bit of trademark research. You can have a great company name, but if someone else owns the trademark on it, you can't claim it. For this, I would hire a trademark attorney to check, but there is also an online search system that you can start with.

The perfect name for your business—whether you are a freelancer, a coach, or are opening a large corporate business—will be a part of your brand's face. When you choose your name wisely, you set the stage for a recognizable brand and company identity for years to come.

3 Brand Strategy: What's Included in a Brand Strategy and Why You Need One

Brand strategy is a long-term plan for your business that will help you achieve your goals by allowing you to position yourself as an expert in your field. Whether you offer services or sell products, and regardless of your status as a freelancer, solopreneur, or owner of a company with employees, you need a brand strategy.

Before you even start to think about hiring a designer to help you with a logo design, website, or any other visual piece, you need to develop a strategy for it. The same thing is true before you start thinking about social media posts, copy for your website, or business cards. You need a plan to know what to do and when to do it. You cannot just randomly pick a mark and call it a logo or randomly write a blog post and say it's for your potential customers.

Brand strategy is a road map that you need to follow in order to get your business where you want it to be. Brand strategy helps you with staying on track and knowing exactly how to use your brand and everything your business can offer. You won't need to guess what your focus should be while you're trying to grow. You won't need to think how to stand out every time, how to find your ideal clients, what to do about the content, if you should redesign your website, or anything else—you will have a plan, you won't waste your time, and you will just do what's stated in the plan.

Brand strategy is "internal branding" of your brand. It helps you define what attributes your brand should have, what emotions it evokes, what the customers' needs are, and how to help them solve problems they are facing. When you have a solid brand strategy in place, you will be able to easily position your brand, clearly demonstrate what your company provides, and show how you are different (and better!) than your competitors.

Since you're already reading this book, I'm sure you know how important branding is in today's world. We have a lot of noise from all the different social media platforms, advertisements, blogs, books, websites, posters on the streets, and billboards—there are so many ways to promote a business. With that in mind, how do you know what to do with yours?

Based on a well-defined brand strategy, you will know where your potential clients are and you will know how to find them, reach out to them, and make them believe in you and eventually invest in you.

Developing a brand strategy can be one of the most difficult steps when starting a business. It can be even harder if you already have a business and now you need to either go back to develop the brand strategy or you need to completely rebrand and start from scratch. Bear with me here. Even though it's challenging, your brand strategy will explain who you are, what you stand for, what you offer, and who your customers or clients are, so it's worth the effort. Your brand strategy will save you time and money in the future because it will target your marketing and advertising efforts toward the people who actually want to purchase from you. When you create your brand strategy, you're really creating your brand's personality. So yes, the process will take a little bit of time, but make it as fun and interesting as you can. You are developing characteristics for an imagined person (business)—how often do you get to do something as creative as that?!

Besides brand strategy, a business should have a business strategy as well. Actually, a brand strategy is similar to, but also forms part of, a business plan. Your business strategy is how your business should operate, while your brand strategy is how your business will appear to other people. It is a process of creating what you want other people to think about your business so they can invest in it and your business can scale.

Business strategy is focused on how a business will make money. It has all the financial plans, the detailed marketing plan, how many people will be on your team, what those people would do, and an overview of the operations of a company. Your business strategy is often communicated through your business plan. Your business plan document can be very broad, and it typically contains a lot of details about the business.

While we won't go into too much detail about business plans in this book, I will quickly cover a few aspects of your business plan that will affect your brand strategy. Your business plan will start with your mission and vision statement.

Your mission is a description of what your business does. For example, let's look at Amazon—a giant company that has a clear mission and vision. Amazon's mission is: "We strive to offer our customers the lowest possible prices, the best available selection, and the utmost convenience."

Your vision is what you want your business to be. It's why your company exists in the first place. Amazon's official vision is: "To be Earth's most customer-centric company, where customers can find and discover anything they might want to buy online."

In addition to a mission and a vision, a business plan will have a value statement that explains your business and brand's priorities and core beliefs. I'm not sure what Amazon's value statement is, but the value statement for my company is, "Strategy and memorable design to scale your brand."

Finally, you will need to identify a goal for your business.

A lot of people are afraid of the word "goal" and are not sure about it. I understand. It's not easy to come up with a goal, but you need to have at least one. Having a clear goal helps you picture the end result of all of your efforts and stay focused on where you're headed while you work step-by-step on your brand and your business. Your goal can be how much money you will make, how many projects you will have, or how many sales (no matter how much money per sale) you will make. But in order to be an effective goal, it needs to be measurable. "I'm going to write" is not a measurable goal, but "I'm going to write one 500-word blog post this week" is a specific goal that you can achieve or fail. Our lives constantly change and, as a result, our life's goals also change. The same is true with business. It doesn't matter if your goal needs to change in the future, but at least try to develop a goal for now. (The next chapter is "Brand Goals" where you will choose one goal for your business and focus your efforts on achieving the goal though a developed step-by-step plan.)

So, brand strategy is how to build a brand in order to grow a business, while business strategy is how to build a business. They both have some elements that overlap and that is how it should be, so don't worry if you are not sure about some sections. These strategies are really important, so it is important to explain them in some detail here.

Brand strategy will help you with your brand's consistency, recognition, trust, and loyalty. Without a brand strategy, you wouldn't have a direction for your brand, and you wouldn't know where your business is going (your goal).

Having a brand strategy in place means you will know a lot about your competitors, and you will know how to stand out and grow your business. You will identify your target audience so you will know how to build your brand identity.

You've probably heard this before, but you will need to create a persona—one person who represents your ideal customer or client—rather than try to appeal to a lot of people. And it's not enough just to know who that "one" person is, but you will need to figure out what she needs, what her struggles are, what she is frustrated with, and then be able to solve her problem and help her. Even if you already know exactly who your persona is and who your competitors are, you might need to dig deeper in order to better separate your brand from others in the same industry, find your niche, define your unique voice, and stand out visually to entice people to choose you! We, as people, can always improve. Our businesses can too.

A brand strategy is essential because your branding expresses your core business values, and if we're not sure what those values are or how to communicate them, our target audience won't be sure either. It is easier and better to "compete" with your competitors based on the value you provide than based on the cheapest price.

For example, Starbucks would never be what it is today if they didn't develop a strong brand strategy first. If Starbucks tried to compete with the cheap gas station coffee—if they were just trying to be cheaper instead of better—they would have failed. Instead, Starbucks built value (quality and consistency) through their brand and stuck to what they did best. They did not care about other coffee companies, and they just focused on the quality they could provide. Having a clear strategy and plan for your brand will generate the consistency that helps you be remembered and recommended to other people—and that's how you scale.

A lot of startups and solopreneurs forget about branding or push it to the side at first. With all the stress and moving pieces that go into launching a business, some entrepreneurs treat branding with the attitude of, "I'll do it later. I just need to start." The problem is that without coming up with a brand strategy, it will be very difficult to build awareness of your company, reach your potential clients, and make sales at all. Even if you find that one perfect buyer, how will he remember and recommend your company when you don't have anything that can be remembered?

The whole point of branding is to either scale your business or to make your business stable in the first place. And having a clear brand strategy for your business will allow you to easily make decisions for your business and keep you moving in the direction of your business goals. Even if your brand strategy isn't perfect, even if you change it down the road based on what your audience responds to, that's fine, change it. But always *have it*.

Sometimes business owners are so focused on the details of what they provide or the precise mechanisms of how their product works, that they haven't stopped to understand what their potential customers are actually looking for. While these details might be important for the back end, they're probably not the marketing points that impress your target customers and get the money in the door. People will engage with you, trust you, and ultimately do business with you based on your brand, and when you target your branding to address the pain points that people have, you will resonate with your audience.

Imagine Apple with no branding. Imagine a world where Apple still provided every single product and service they do now, but with no visual consistency or content strategy whatsoever. How would you remember who they were if they didn't have their logo, well-designed stores, inspiring commercials, and impeccable website? All of Apple's offerings look consistent — their stores, products, and websites all have a minimalistic look with grey tones, and everything contains useful information.

Your brand strategy also dictates your marketing strategy. Once you have clarity around who your target is, what they need, how you are different from your competitors, what your tone is, and how you communicate with potential consumers, you will know where to find customers or make your brand visible and accessible so they can find you. You will know if your website needs improvement, or if you need to invest in Google ads, direct marketing, or other methods of advertising. So, before you start investing in social media, logo design, or a website, you need to be clear on what your brand is, how it sounds to others, and what the qualities are.

Your company's purpose will also be defined by the brand strategy. Some people would say that the purpose of their business is to be successful, make a certain amount of money, or simply sell a specific product or provide a service. But that's just what your company *does* and not its *purpose*. A purpose needs to be way deeper than your services or products. People resonate better with brands that want to help and provide support. IKEA's purpose isn't just to sell furniture, but to "create a better everyday life." And people resonate with that—customers want to feel that better life and invest in it. By having a purpose, IKEA provides more value than just selling furniture.

What's the purpose of your business? Take a moment to really consider why your business exists and what problem you are trying to solve. For example: My company provides brand strategy and design, but my company's *purpose* is to scale other people's businesses by connecting potential consumers with their brand.

Your brand strategy will help your business establish consistency. You need a consistent voice and look across all platforms—all of your text, images, and other content should have a similar look, feel, voice, and tone. Remember, you are talking to the same target audience wherever your business can be found.

Without a brand strategy, your business will not have a roadmap so you will not know which direction it should go.

Once, I was at a networking event and met a woman who had an amazing product. She had towels in all different shapes, colors, and fabrics. I loved it so much that I purchased a few immediately. After I told her that I was a brand strategist, we started to talk about her business, and she said that she wanted to make more online sales. She was great at making sales in person, but her conversion rate (number of actual sales) on her website was really low even though her website looked good. She was right. She did have a nice website, but that was it. It was all about the look. She didn't make a connection with potential buyers. The website didn't have an engaging story with compelling text, her photos were random, and there wasn't a clear call to action. In other words, it was a nice website with no purpose.

How did this happen? She was missing a brand strategy. A strategically designed website will make more money than a good-looking website every time. We'll talk about this more in Chapter 13: Designs For Your Business.

What is included in a brand strategy and how can you create your own?

Brand strategy is more important than the visual design. How is that even possible when people see only the "outside" of a business (the logo, website, or business cards)? The answer is that successful designs are based on a brand strategy. If you let your brand strategy dictate your design, then your visual designs will be attractive to your target audience.

Since a full brand strategy document includes quite a bit of information, I always recommend that business owners break their brand strategies down into smaller and more manageable sections. I like to separate branding into internal and external categories so that entrepreneurs and business owners can understand it easier. In general, internal branding is the strategy and external branding is the design and execution. Sounds really easy, but let's dive deeper into the differences between internal and external branding.

Internal branding includes brand discovery, brand positioning and competitor analysis, target profiles (customer needs & emotions), brand attributes & voice, content strategy, and goals. We will go through each step in this book.

External branding includes logo design, website, stationery design, search engine optimization (SEO), blogging, social media, ads, and marketing.

Brand discovery is always the first step in internal branding. Here you will write down as much as you can about your business. You should write down when and how you started your business (or when and how you will start one), what made you decide to start it, how much money you plan to spend on it, and what your goal is for the business. Brand discovery is more important when you hire a brand strategist and designer than if you are trying to define your business by yourself (because you already should know why and how you are planning on starting your business).

Brand positioning and competitor analysis is where you set your business apart from the competitors. Who are your most important competitors? Which ones are the closest, the most competitive, and the most similar? These are your direct competitors. Discover what you can about each one—what are their strengths and weaknesses, are they growing or struggling, and what kind of messaging do they have? Then, try to figure out what differentiates you from these competitors. Why would people choose you over them? What do you offer that's different? Find your unique selling proposition and brand promise. (There will be more about this in Chapter 6, about brand positioning.)

Brand attributes & voice are the characteristics that describe your brand. You should aim to have two or three key words that evoke the image of your brand. Here is a simple exercise to describe your brand attributes: Imagine that your brand is a person, and then just try to describe that person. Maybe your brand is smart, inventive, and friendly (Microsoft). Maybe your brand is disruptive, cutting-edge, and defiant (Uber). It's basically making your brand look and feel how you want your potential consumers to think and feel about your brand. Brand voice is also a component of your brand attributes, since your brand voice affects how your content will sound to the public. We will cover much more in Chapter 7: Brand Attributes.

When we talk about **user profiles or target market**, that's when you identify your potential customers or clients. Not just in a sense of how old they are, where they live, and what gender they are, but also what they want, what kind of problems they have, and how you can solve those problems. The whole brand you are creating is for them, not for you. More about this in Chapter 5: User Profiles.

Goal setting is the process of setting your business goals. It's not your weekly or monthly goals—it's your two-, five- and even ten-year goals. Most of the time business goals are measured in revenue—how much money a business will make in a year or five years. Then chop that into pieces and make a plan on what needs to be done every year, every month, and every day in order to accomplish those goals. There are also brand goals. Depending on your business, your brand will have goals and plans on how to reach a potential client, and what it needs to do in order to be visible and in front of the right people. In this book, our focus is on branding and, with that, brand goals. You will learn exactly how to set up your goals by reading Chapter 4: Brand Goals and Objectives.

Content strategy is basically writing for your target. It's figuring out what they would like to hear, what resonates with them, and how they can connect and engage with your brand. For example, my ideal clients are startups and entrepreneurs. They love learning about businesses, scaling companies, and financial growth, so those are the topics I write about. You will learn how to develop your content strategy in Chapter 8: Content Strategy. After you develop a content strategy, the next step is execution—and execution falls under external branding.

The easiest definition of external branding is: External branding includes everything that people can see. Your website, logo, typography, and social media posts are all part of your external branding. Once you have your content strategy, once you know the audience you are writing for and how to speak to them effectively, you would implement that strategy in your social media, email marketing, and website copy. Also, once you have all the brand attributes (such as luxury, smart, clean, and so on), you will know how your visual branding should look. You will know if your logo is the right one for your company, and you will know if your website fits your company's vision based on the look and feel that it has.

So, how do you create the brand strategy, you ask? Well, first you need to step back. What do you want? This is not just a big business goal; it's more a life goal. What do you want for your life? Where do you see yourself in five or ten years? Do you see yourself as an owner of an online business, as a location-independent entrepreneur, or as the owner of a brick-and-mortar business? Do you have employees or are you a solopreneur? And what will you need to do or make to get there?

After you have thought about those things, take a moment to step even further outside of your company, business, or idea. Look at it as if you are a friend to a person who wants to make that business idea work. Do you have any advice for that friend? Think about it. The advice needs to be on a level of someone who is not that knowledgeable about the nitty-gritty details of your industry. The advice can be, "Go and find a business coach to help you. I don't know much about it. I've never started a business before," and this might resonate with you. Your advice might be, "Go and hire a designer to help you design eye-catching business cards so you're ready for networking events," or it might be, "You need to work 16 hours a day to make that work." What perspective would an outsider have about your business at this point on your journey?

After you know where you want to be and what "your friend" told you he thinks you should do for your business, you are ready to start working on your branding. It's easy. Just follow the steps, chapter by chapter, and before you know it, you will really own your brand. So, let's start putting your brand together piece by piece.

4 Brand Goals & Objectives

Businesses have the goal of creating a recognizable and successful brand in order to grow. In this chapter, we will discuss how to set brand goals that will align with your existing business goals. As we discussed earlier, brand goals are not the same as business goals, but these two types of goals are connected and related to each other. Both goals need to be clear and easy to understand, but most importantly, you need to have a plan for how to accomplish both your brand and business goals, and how you will measure your success. In order to be effective, goals must be realistic, specific, and measurable.

"A goal without a plan is just a wish." – Antoine de Saint-Exupéry

Business goals describe what a company expects to accomplish over a specific period of time. For example, if your goal is to make $100,000 this year in your business, you will need a certain number of clients or sales to reach that goal by the end of the year. $100,000 divided by 12 months is $8,333 per month. What will you need to do to reach that monthly revenue number? How many clients will you need to serve? How many products will you need to sell? Whatever those numbers are, that is now your business goal.

Brand goals describe what a company expects to accomplish with its branding over a specific period of time. In order to create a successful brand, your branding needs to have a concrete goal and a brand strategy for it. You will learn how to start creating your brand strategy in the next chapter, but for now just think of a brand strategy like it's a business plan—but *specifically* focused on the branding itself. Everything that we see, hear, and know about a company comes from its branding. Whether that branding takes the shape of the company's logo, theme song, video, stories from people who are familiar with the company, website, colors, or anything else, those branding elements were created on purpose to evoke a specific *feeling* from customers.

Branding goals are very similar to business goals, and there are a few guidelines that will help you set effective brand goals. First, there has to be a reason behind everything you are doing with your brand. Second, you need to be really specific in your plans about what you are trying to accomplish. Otherwise, you will just waste your time and money and you will not see the growth in your business. Your to-do list will be based on these brand goals that you set, and you will know what to focus on and what priorities and actions you need to take so you can get your business to the level you desire. And it can all be done through a strategic plan instead of guessing what the next step should and could be.

To understand **the value of a powerful brand**, let's look again at Coca-Cola and what the company has done with branding. When someone mentions Coca-Cola, what is the very first thought that comes to your mind? You probably think of their logo or their nickname "Coke." If you think more about it, you will probably think about their ads related to Christmas, New Year's Eve, Santa, family, friends, a nice and warm home environment—it's all connected. If I were going to describe their branding in one word, I would say "happiness." Now, I don't know their business goals, but I see how they are creating a positive impression on consumers by using the right branding. They didn't use their red color by accident or create ads randomly. It's all well-planned.

If you want to reach any goal, you have to constantly work on following your brand plans and the steps to achieve your brand goals. Each step needs to be related with the previous one, and you need to set up priorities. This is where it helps to separate your goals from your objectives. These words sound similar and we often mix them up—they both are things that need to be done in order to achieve something.

Objectives are like small goals inside one goal. Think of objectives as the specific steps that a business needs to take in order to get to the main goal. **Goals** can be broad while objectives are narrow and specific. Both have a certain time frame. For example, if you want to build a website (goal), you need to create one page at a time (objectives).

We use goals and objectives in our daily lives all the time. Even making a pot of tea has a goal (drink tea) and objectives (boil the water, take a cup, put a tea bag into a cup, pour the water over the bag, wait for a few minutes...). Once you know your brand goals, you can break them into pieces and create a plan. All the steps in that plan will be objectives. To summarize: Goals are your aspirations while objectives are your to-do list.

It is very important to have objectives because they will help you stay on the right track. If you don't have a plan for how to accomplish a certain goal, it will be really difficult to accomplish it, and you run the risk of wasting time on tasks that will not directly lead to your goal.

When it comes to branding, the five major brand goals are:

- Build awareness.
- Create an emotional connection.
- Differentiate your offering.
- Create credibility and trust.
- Motivate purchasing.

Before deciding what your brand goal should be, you need to ask yourself what you are trying to achieve through branding. What do you need in order to get people to purchase your product or services? Every company's branding needs all of the five major brand goals because every business needs to build awareness, people need to trust you, they need to be connected and engaged, and they need a reason or motivation to make a purchase. You will work on all of the goals, but I suggest you pick one that you will concentrate your focus on for the next three to six months.

When you focus on one goal, you can break it into steps and have a plan for how to get where you want your business to be. If your goal is to differentiate, you will still build awareness by showing your brand. If you want to create an emotional connection, you will still create credibility and trust by engaging with your target and so on. All of these brand goals are connected, but having a focus will accelerate your results.

1. Building awareness for a brand means increasing brand recognition, either offline or online. With this strategy and brand goal in mind, a business is trying to reach as many people as it can and do it again and again. Potential customers are able to recall and recognize the brand because they already saw it a few times and remember it. After that, they feel like they know enough about the brand and are ready to learn more, eventually getting closer to the brand to make a purchase.

Brand awareness is important because it helps businesses stand out from their competition, build an audience more effectively, and generate more leads. You know how people say that people buy from people that they know, like, and trust? It's the same with brands. People will buy from your brand if they know about it, like it, and can trust the product or services your business is offering. But they need to know about you first.

Every business is building brand awareness, no matter if that was the focus (goal) or not, but depending on the type and size of your business, building awareness might not be the right goal for you right away. Mercedes, Pepsi, Gucci, and other big brands do this constantly. We are all aware of those brands, but this is a goal for which you need to have a certain budget in mind because most of the time this is done through advertising and social media marketing.

Brand recognition is built through brand awareness as well. How many times have you seen an ad for McDonalds? You know exactly what they offer, and you might even know their pricing as well. You will always recognize their colors, their golden arches that are meant to be reminiscent of the letter M, and even their menu.

There is no strategy for how to build brand recognition faster. Your brand simply needs to constantly be in front of people for a long time. Besides the ads and marketing I mentioned above, you can find people who will help you promote your business, or create referral programs, print your logo on pens, or do social media contests. The strategy with brand awareness is to reach out to as many people as possible.

If your startup needs revenue immediately, building brand awareness is not going to be the right choice for you. It can take years of constantly creating content (either text or images), doing promotions, and reaching out to people before seeing any results. Brand awareness is worth it in the long run, and big brands do it, but if you don't have years to spare in the beginning, then your focus should be on something else.

2. Creating an emotional connection starts with storytelling. Storytelling consists of stories that resonate with the target. That doesn't mean that the story needs to be personal and private, such as Himalayan salt helped you with your blood pressure and now you are selling packages of Himalayan salt and want to help other people, but you can create a unique story for your brand. Car companies always have stories about how and why their products are safe, and they have stories that people resonate with, such as driving with a family member or going for a vacation.

However, creating an emotional connection is not for all businesses and brands. Do you remember the last time you bought a sponge for your dishes? You looked at the sponges, saw packaging, glanced at pricing, and bought the one that made the most sense in that moment. You may not even remember what company made it. On the other hand, imagine buying sunglasses. This is where emotions come into play—sunglasses marketing is all about making people feel good about their decisions. You might feel good about buying the right sponge too, but not in the same way that you for sure feel good about buying the right sunglasses, and that's because you made an emotional connection.

Do your clients need to feel good about your services or products? Most of the time the answer is yes, but you need to figure out if this goal will be your focus. To create an emotional connection, your business will need to create a lot of content—content that tells stories and speaks to your potential clients in a way they understand. The content will be textual and visual as well.

Through text, you can directly express your brand's feelings, as if your brand were a person, and through visuals you can connect it even more to the potential buyers. Colors will be included as well. All colors have different meanings (which we will cover later in this book), and the photos you use in your branding can be related to your target—such as a businesswoman, family, something simple and beautiful, nature etc., depending on who you're trying to speak to.

You create an emotional connection between your brand and your target in the same way that you create a connection with your friends—don't push it, don't force it, make it feel natural, talk with them, be there for them when they need you, reach out when you need them, and just let your brand and business be what they are. When you can effectively and naturally communicate this to your customers, people will resonate, connect, and make a decision to buy based on the relationships you created with them.

3. Differentiating your product or services means trying to stand out from the competitors and highlighting those differences. We will go through this process and you will learn how to separate yourself from the crowd in Chapter 6: Brand Positioning, but this is a very focused and strategic goal that can be accomplished via analyzing your competitors first.

The easiest way to differentiate your company is to find that one thing that makes you different. Is it the reason why you started your business, is it the extra service you provide, is it the convenience, is it the location, or is it the price? Whatever it might be, you need to use that thing all the time in your content, on your website, in your flyers, etc. Customers need to see your offering as unique and different in a good way. They need to answer to themselves, "Why would I choose this brand over any other that provides similar services or product?" When they understand why you are different, they will have a clear reason to buy from you.

4. When people invest in something, they need to be sure it's the right move for them. They need to believe that the product or services they are purchasing is providing the quality they expect. In order to **create credibility and trust**, a business needs to look established, professional, and appealing to potential clients. For many small brands, consistently creating relationships and keeping the same communication style can develop a deeper level of trust. Some businesses require networking in person; some require an online presence such as social media. However, you need to find your way of talking to people, engaging, communicating, and building a long-lasting relationship with them.

This brand goal is extremely important to understand, even if you don't set it as your main goal. Just think for a second: you, like everyone else, prefer to buy things from people that you can trust and people that can really help you. Trust is built via word of mouth, client referrals, and partners in real life, or online by positioning yourself as an expert in your field, creating tutorials, writing educational articles, and sharing them through social media.

Depending on your type of business, you can choose this as your goal and then break this goal into objectives such as asking clients for testimonials, writing two educational blogs a month, or going to one networking event per week.

If you are in the service industry, you can prove that you're an expert by creating an online course, becoming a speaker, or writing an e-book. All of these things can serve as proof to people that you are knowledgeable and that you can help them. If you are in the retail industry, you can always write educational articles about the product you are trying to sell and set yourself as an expert that way.

5. **Motivate purchasing** is for brands and business that have existed for some time and already have a high level of brand awareness. Usually these brands motivate purchasing through offering discounts or some other "sales push." You can actually try to motivate someone to purchase your product or service using any of the above five goals. You might motivate someone to invest in your brand by connecting your story with them, maybe by explaining how you are different

than your competitors, or maybe by displaying your customers' reviews (which demonstrate credibility and trust). If motivating purchasing is your main brand goal, focus on the objectives—what specifically will motivate them to purchase your offerings?

It's a really thin line between all these brand goals, and no matter which goal you choose as your main focus, you will end up making progress on all of these goals as you move forward through *BrandFix*. For example, any actions you take to motivate purchasing will naturally increase your brand awareness as well—even if brand awareness wasn't the primary focus.

If you are just launching a brand, I recommend that you choose to **create an emotional connection** or **differentiate your product** as your focus goal. And if you have a large budget to spend on your new brand, then I would also recommend building **brand awareness**.

If you are already in business, I suggest you choose to **create credibility and trust** or **motivate purchasing** as your focus goal.

Once you have a business goal, a brand goal, and corresponding objectives, you can put these concepts together. Here is an example of what it looks like to combine these goals:

- Business Goal: Our business needs to make $50,000 by the end of July.
- Brand Goal: We need to create an emotional connection so people can relate to us, trust us, and purchase our product.

- Objectives: To accomplish these goals, we need to write one blog post a week, attend three networking events per month, finish our promotional video (storytelling), and redesign our website.

Now that you have decided on your primary brand goal and created your objectives, we can move on to creating your overarching brand strategy that will influence every aspect of your branding.

5 Target Profiles

You have probably heard that every business needs to have an ideal client. But what does that actually mean? And how can that help your business?

One of my main mottos sentences when it comes to business operation is "It's about them, not you." Business owners sometimes don't understand that. Often, they create a brand that they like personally, but they don't consider who their target audience is and whether their brand will appeal to that audience. You may already have a general understanding of who your target is, but imagine if you knew that your target is Rachel who is 29 years old, works from home, lives in Central Austin, Texas, feels lonely, and likes to eat lunch at XYZ restaurant.

If you knew that *Rachel* was your target, rather than every single person who works from home, you could walk right into XYZ restaurant and leave flyers so she would see them. You could create content on Instagram that speaks directly to Rachel so she is drawn to your posts. That doesn't mean you are targeting one single person, but you are targeting your ideal client. All "Rachels" who are out there will resonate with the content you're putting in front of them, and you are getting your foot in the door.

Rather than targeting everyone, you need to know which people are most likely to purchase your product or invest in your services, and you need to put your business in front of them. Not everyone is interested in what you have to offer, so why waste your time and money on trying to do something that is not going to bring you success? Targeting specific people is much more effective, efficient, and affordable than being all over the place.

Small businesses often make this mistake by thinking that by targeting a specific person they are excluding the rest. Not at all! You are just simply attracting the right people—the people who want what you offer.

Your business's focus will be on your target. Your brand is for them and your business exists because of them—it is not for you. Your message, your voice, and your visuals (such as your logo and website), are all created for that person. Furthermore, your social media posts should involve things your target finds interesting—everything is made for them. In my work as a designer and brand strategist, I often hear from business owners, "I don't like that color, I prefer this color," but in the end it won't be our own personal favorite colors that attract customers. Once I ask, "What color would your target prefer?" they realize that we are branding a business in a way that will attract *other* people to it, not something that would attract just the business owner. Yes, every business owner wants to like their brand, but the sooner you can get out of the mindset of "What do I like?" and into the mindset of "What does my target customer like?" the more effective your branding will be.

The most important thing (the base) is identifying whether your business is business-to-consumer (B2C) or business-to-business (B2B). If you are selling directly to people, your company is B2C. Common examples of B2C businesses are clothing stores, coffee shops, essential oil businesses, and art- or craft-based businesses. You are targeting individual people who need your services or products, not other businesses.

On the other hand, if you are selling to other businesses, your company is B2B. For example, if you are a commercial realtor or you have developed software that other companies can purchase, you are targeting businesses rather than individuals. When it comes to finding your target, B2B brands require a different strategy than B2C brands, so it's important to figure out now which category your company falls into.

Let's talk about B2C targets first, then we'll talk about B2B targets. Whichever your business might be, I recommend you read both parts because they support each other even though they have different strategies.

Finding Your Target Customers: For B2C Brands

The first step is to look at your current customers (if you have them). Who are they? What do they need and how do you help them? Why do they buy from you?

If your business is not active yet, start by determining your ideal customer's (target) demographic. Who do you want your business to serve? Identify your ideal customer's gender, age, location, occupation, education, income, marital status, and whether they have children. Knowing this information, you will be able to picture who that person is. You will know what their day-to-day life is like, what is important to them, and if they hang out online or offline and on which sites.

Of course, you will not be able to use all this information when targeting and writing copy for them, so you will need to use core markets and secondary markets. **The core market** is the primary market—the most important bit of information. Do you need to target people who are a certain age, have a particular occupation, or are in a specific location? The core market is that **one** most important thing. Just choose one thing on which you would want to focus. **The secondary market** is the second-most important characteristic about your target. So, for example, you can choose occupation as your primary market and location as your secondary market. Maybe that then leads you to graphic designers in Austin, which is way easier to target than all creatives in the USA, right? Or you can have two core markets (maximum) like 25-34 years old (age) and $40,000–$50,000 (income) a year, and your secondary market can be men (gender).

When you know what your target demographic is (defined by the core and secondary markets), you should then focus on the psychographic of your target. Figure out why those people would invest in your services or product. **The target demographic is the "who" of who you are helping, and the psychographic is the "why" that causes them to spend**

money with your brand. The psychographic helps a lot—more than demographics—when identifying how to communicate with your target and create content that will resonate with them. The psychographic includes not just the "why" of your target but their **behavior** as well. Once you know what they like, what they don't like, what their interests are, and what they are passionate about, you can create content and visuals that will inspire them to invest in your services or products.

For example, our ideal client Rachel is 29 years old, lives in Central Austin, and works from home—that's her demographic. But the fact that she will become a member of my coworking space because she feels lonely at home, likes to collaborate with other entrepreneurs, and needs high-speed internet in order to send projects to her clients—that's her psychographic.

To dig into the psychographic of your potential customers, you can do more than just brainstorm and randomly come up with reasons why someone would contact you. There is actually a process of knowing the psychographics of your customers, which I call *monitoring your target market's interests.*

Do you know what interests your potential customers have? What are their beliefs, attitudes, behaviors, and hobbies? To discover these you need to put yourself in their shoes and imagine that *you* are that Rachel who works from home every day. What does Rachel like about working from home? And even more importantly, what does she hate about it? What has she already done to try to solve her problem of feeling lonely all the time?

Try to imagine what a week in the life of your potential client looks like. Then try to imagine one of their days. From morning, lunch, talking to their family and friends, to exercising or doing something else, and going to bed. This can be challenging because it requires you to put yourself in someone else's shoes, but just keep in mind that it's crucial to understand the personality of your target persona so you can talk directly to them. You need to know as much as you can about them.

Once you have an inside-out understanding of what makes your target tick, choose two or three of their activities and focus on those. You will not be able to target someone with six interests, but you could choose one or two and use those to attract them.

When you are B2C, it's important to pay attention to the behaviors of your potential target. It might occur to you that your target doesn't just like yoga but also loves to swim. You might realize that your target is not someone who is 25 years old but someone who is 35. The point is, you can always change your messaging or your target as needed.

You can refine your target audience by getting feedback from customers. Ask them if they have purchased a similar product before or had services that are similar to yours. If they did, find out what they liked and didn't like. See if you can discover other things as well—what their major concerns were, how satisfied they were at the end, and what is the biggest hesitation they have when they think about buying. Focus on those concerns and use them in your messaging. For example: If you discover that customers are afraid that your sunscreen might dry their skin, you can mention "our products do not cause dry skin" or "our products moisturize skin" in your messaging. That way, you eliminate their "don't buy" voice in their heads and help them trust the product.

Dive deep into their problems. What are they? How did they get those problems? How do they feel about them? Once you know their concerns, you can help them out. Don't think just about your business and making money by selling your product or services, but really think about how to be helpful and how to make customers feel happy, satisfied, and better after interacting with your brand.

Now that you have identified your target, you just need to adjust your messaging to focus on them. From the tone of your brand to your visual identity, website copy, and advertising, everything is specific to your target. Once you talk directly to them, it is more likely that they will connect with you. Your offer will resonate with them and they will buy it. Learn how to communicate with them. Show them how you are solving their problems. For example, using the sunscreen example above, you could ask, "Do you have dry skin? This product can help you because..."

Be conversational. Imagine you are talking to a friend and just write that down. Speaking to your audience really can be that simple, as long as you resist the urge to overcomplicate it. For example, when people go to my website, I explain exactly what I offer, how I do it, and that I can help their businesses grow by connecting their business to the right target audience.

And now, the most important part: Determine how your potential customer will learn about you. How can you get in front of them? Remember the example about putting flyers in front of Rachel where she goes for lunch? Based on the interests, demographics, and psychographics you outlined above, start to make a list of where exactly your potential customers are right now. If your customers are online, you could reach them by investing in Facebook ads, Twitter ads, or other online platforms. If your customers are in gyms or grocery stores close to your location, make flyers with messages for them. Work on your list the whole time while reading this book, and once you develop your brand strategy and get to the chapter "Strategic Elements," you will know 100% what you need to do!

Finding Your Target Customers: For B2B Brands

If your business is B2B, you will need to target other businesses in order to sell your products or services.

B2B customers are harder to define because you need to know what businesses can benefit from your services or products. From there you will need to identify the company's size and who the decision makers are in the company, and then get in front of those people. Who would be the person responsible for deciding whether or not to purchase from you?

Unlike B2C, a lot of people need to benefit from you. You're not targeting one person who has a problem you can solve and make happy. Instead, you need to have a strategic approach so that the whole business you are targeting can be "happy."

With B2C, after you know who your target is, you make a decision on how to get in front of them and you can jump right in. With B2B, you might have to make presentations to a team of people, so you need a complete strategic marketing plan.

The first step to finding your target, as a B2B brand, is to think about what you offer and make sure you are crystal clear with what your offering does for other businesses. When I was starting off as a designer, I wanted to make brand boards for companies. A brand board is a document that contains your company's logo, web and print fonts, color codes, and images. But the major problem was that companies didn't know the term "brand board," so even though a brand board could have helped them immensely, they didn't understand what I was selling and thus decided they didn't need one.

In retrospect, I could have sold more brand boards if I had used words that my target understood. I could have said, "Do you know your brand's colors? What fonts do you use?" or something similar. So, you need to know both what you offer and how to describe that to your target in a way they can understand. And then you need to come up with a reason why they would purchase from you. For example: "If you would like to have *more free time*, use this software to schedule all your social media posts."

Next, you need to define the audience. To do this, you need information about the business you are trying to communicate with. Does it have two or five or 50 employees? The size of your target company matters because when you know their structure and who does what in the company, you will know the person (or job title) you need to approach. If a company has two employees, you are most likely going to talk directly with the owner when discussing your services. But if you want to work with a company like Walmart, you're definitely not going to meet with the company owner. In that case, you would work with a manager or someone from their marketing or business department who in turn would present the idea to someone above them. When you have an idea of what sized companies you would like to target, you can organize your efforts appropriately.

For example: My company offers brand strategy and design to companies and brands, which means I am B2B. I serve either startups with a few stakeholders or businesses that are growing so they need to rebrand. Most of the time, the owners don't look for a brand strategist or designer by themselves, but they direct an internal marketing person who works for the company to find me. This marketing person is my "in" to the company, and typically this person is someone who oversees and directs marketing efforts to reach the company's goals of promoting and scaling, but they don't actually design logos, run ads, or create videos. Since I am so clear that I'm targeting people who do marketing for companies, I find people who meet that description by going to networking events and creating relationships with them in person.

Just Talk to Your Target

To summarize: Define if you're B2C or B2B first, and then make a plan for how to get in front of your target based on who your target is. Once you know where to find them, your next step is to create content and *visuals for them*. (Remember, their opinion and preferences matter the most!) Your blog posts, articles, flyers, testimonials you previously received, website, social media posts, ads—everything your business or brand produces needs to speak to your target audience so they can resonate with your message and then make a purchase.

Once you have a clear idea on what you offer and what problems you are solving, and you have identified who has those problems and where those people or businesses are, you can start to work on brand positioning.

6 Brand Positioning

Brand positioning is the strategy of setting a business apart from the competition. It describes how a brand is different from other brands that offer the same or similar services or products. **It's a process of positioning a brand into consumer's minds.** When you position your brand, you influence what people think first when your brand comes to their mind — and that needs to be different from what they think about your competitors that offer the same thing.

To position your brand, it's important to be clear on what sets your company apart from your competition. Is it your "why?" Is it how and where you started your business?

Most people didn't start their companies just for fun. They usually have a reason, such as they wanted to do something better, or they couldn't find a service or product, so they created it themselves, or they just wanted to build something that was different and unique. Even when two businesses seem almost exactly alike, there is always room for a branding-savvy entrepreneur to differentiate one company's products and services from the other's.

Each brand and business is different. As a business owner, you need to know what makes your business different and how to communicate that difference to your potential consumers. Your business needs to build a personality that will have its own voice and identity.

Your brand positioning is more than a name, logo, colors, clever tagline, or website. It's the "what" that's different from other businesses in the same industry. You will know your brand positioning is effective when people say, "This company is the best because of XYZ."

You already have experience with brand positioning, even if you don't realize it yet. For example: Every hair stylist knows how to cut hair, but perhaps you go to the same stylist every time. Why? What is it about your stylist that makes you keep coming back?

And which do you like better—McDonald's or Burger King? Okay, you may not even like fast food, but this is an example of two companies that are *extremely* similar, offering almost the same food, prices, and services, and yet consumers often have strong opinions over which brand they prefer. The same is true for Uber and Lyft.

Establishing what makes your brand different involves looking into the details of your business and trying to differentiate what you do better than anyone else. What is the reason why someone would choose *you?*

It also involves identifying all the similarities and differences a business has with its competitors. In order to create a better brand image, a brand needs to know all the weaknesses and strengths similar brands have.

Brand positioning is one of the most powerful marketing tactics. In 1957, David Ogilvy used the positioning concept to position Dove as beauty soap for women. By adding the words "beauty" and "for women," he separated the company from other companies and focused on women who wanted to look better. He wasn't offering just another soap but a "beauty soap," and it was just for women. Men could buy it too, but by focusing on a specific gender, he narrowed down his audience and created a niche and specific target. Brand positioning will direct a business to market and advertise its products or services to a target audience using that *differentiator* to stand out.

Clear brand positioning helps a brand effectively communicate and reach its potential consumers. Every day, we see a lot of different advertisements, offers, and discounts, and it can become overwhelming. If a brand wants to grow, their message really needs to stand out. Knowing exactly what your brand offers, who it serves, and what benefits you provide will make your business more efficient. People like making easy decisions; by positioning your brand, you can help them make a fast and easy decision when they are about to purchase your product or contact you for your services.

To position your brand, you need to understand what your customers want, what your capabilities are, and how your competitor is positioning their brand as well. The positioning must be easy to understand and communicate. Without knowing your positioning, what would you write in your copy? It's almost impossible to write about your brand when you don't know where it sits and when you don't recognize your uniqueness. And what would your visual design look like? How can you tell a different story if you don't know your positioning? How would a designer design a professional logo that speaks to your target without knowing what the logo needs to express?

Positioning is really powerful in setting your business up for future success as well. It will help drive growth and build a business that is different from everything that is already out there.

Most of the time your "why" is what sets you apart. There was a reason why you started this company and that reason can be used to help you stand out.

I own a coworking space. Coworking spaces are shared office spaces for entrepreneurs, freelancers, and remote workers — people who otherwise work from home. It's a growing industry and there are a lot of coworking places that are close to mine, so it wasn't easy to differentiate. We all provide desks, coffee, meeting rooms, 24-hour access, and event space. Some coworking spaces have adjustable (sit-to-stand) desks, some have extra monitors, some have lockers, some are focused on the community, but in order to position my space apart from the others, I had to identify that one "wow factor" that separated my brand from the rest.

For me, that differentiation was part of my "why." One of the reasons I opened the coworking space was because I didn't want to be a full-time coworker. I wanted to work from

Brand Positioning

a shared office space—but not every day. I wanted to spend some days at home as well, so I didn't want to pay for five or seven days a week if I was only going to go two or three times a week. Because this was my "why," I purposely designed my coworking space to be ideal for part-time coworkers, and I set up a unique three-days-a-week membership level to serve my niche.

Once my coworking space opened, most of our members chose the three-days-a-week membership option so they can still happily work at home a few days without feeling like they are wasting money. These are my ideal clients, and they found me because I positioned my space as the premier space for part-time coworkers. But, as mentioned, it wasn't easy to distinguish my space initially. I first needed to learn a lot about other spaces to be able to open mine, and from there I positioned my space and communicated that positioning to my target.

Your brand positioning doesn't always have to revolve around a "why." If you have a location-independent lifestyle business, and your "why" was to be independent, then keep in mind that you're not different from your competitors because you're a freelancer. They are all freelancers as well. Your content, your work, quality of your communication—all of that will differentiate you. But even before people reach out to you or purchase your services or products, what did they already like about your brand? Why would they choose you over others? What are your points of difference?

In order to start creating a unique positioning, start with listing all the **capabilities** your brand has.

So if you operate a service company, what are all the services you offer? If you sell a product, what are all the products you are selling? It can be even just one service or one product— that's fine too. It's just that what you offer needs to be defined so it can be compared to your competitors. This seems obvious, but sometimes we get so caught up in running our businesses that we lose sight of what exactly we offer. Write down everything that your company offers. The list most likely will have at least three things or a single thing with three attributes (descriptions). The challenge is always how to present those offerings to a potential client in a different way from what your competitors are already doing.

You also need to know what your mission is, what your values are, and how you can solve other people's problems. Then you can establish exactly who your target is, how old they are, their behavior, their needs, and their challenges. As you go through BrandFix, you will continue to work on all of these segments of your business.

Analyzing Your Competition

The next step in the brand positioning process is identifying your direct competitors. It is incredibly important to analyze your competition. Competitors are not all companies that are in the same industry. Sometimes it depends on the location, services, communication, or product. So, what are direct competitors? Who are they? And how you can identify them?

When I start to work with small business clients, I always ask them who *they* think their competitors are and why. I either get a list of incredibly famous brands that do similar things, or my clients say that they don't have competitors because they think that what they offer is too unique and doesn't exist yet. Most of the time neither is correct.

Not all businesses that are in the same industry are your competitors either. For example, if you're a life coach who is just starting out, Tony Robbins is not your competitor. **Competitors are businesses and brands you are directly competing with.** Maybe one day, when you become as good, as popular, and as well-known as Tony Robbins, you can compete with him. But right now, he is not your competitor. Your competitors would be life coaches focused on the same topic, life coaches just starting out who have similar-sized audiences, people in your networking groups, etc.

If you are a fashion designer who has a local dress boutique close to a Gucci store, Gucci may not be your competitor. Even though both of your brick-and-mortar stores are in a similar location, that doesn't mean you offer the same style, same pricing, or the same customer service. It is really important to understand that not everyone is your competitor because otherwise you will waste so much time trying to compete with companies and people who don't even notice you. Don't go too far. It's a little bit of research, but it's well worth it!

On the other hand, as mentioned, some people would say they don't have competitors at all. They would say they are unique, different, or have a completely new concept that doesn't exist anywhere. Well, that's almost impossible. I had clients tell me they had no competitors, but I already knew who their competitors were. In today's world, there is always competition, but there's room for everyone too. There are always people and companies that provide similar products or services—you just don't know about them. You might not be familiar with those businesses because they don't stand out enough and are not good with branding, marketing, and advertising. Or maybe you are too focused on your idea instead of a similar idea that your potential competitors might offer. No matter what, your competitors do exist.

Once you have identified at least three competitors, think about the specific things that they offer. Not how they market themselves (this comes later) but only what they offer. Look at their products or services in terms of features, value, and quality. Do you offer the same? If so, what can you add as extra value to stand out from them?

There are two options for adding value. One is to lower the price you charge for similar services—something I would not recommend because you will probably sound cheap and inferior, and you'll contribute to undervaluing those types of services for the whole industry. But there's another option: Simply add more value to the same product or service so your consumers spend less money to get more. Think of ways you can offer extra perks and value for your target. Go above and beyond for them. Compete with others on value, not price!

What do your competitors offer that you don't? How can you get around that? Can you maybe add those features as well, or can you add those features *plus* one more thing? Is there anything you can add to your offering that your competitors might not have yet? I added the three-days-a-week membership level to my coworking business because nobody else had it. You need to have something different or extra to stand out.

One useful exercise is to look at each of your competitors as though you are one of their top customers. What do you love about their brand?" What makes them sound really appealing?

What are their strengths? Then ask yourself, what is it that you don't like? It doesn't have to be something bad, but just something that *you* don't like and would not include in your business. Next, compare your visual identity to each of these three competitors. You don't need to do an hours-long analysis of each competitor, but it's important to take a few minutes to explore each competitor's online presence:

- Do your competitors have logos? If so, how would you describe their logos? (Simple, elegant, strong, luxury?)
- What colors do your competitors use? Do you know why?
- Are your competitors' websites easy to navigate? Can you find all the information you need, along with their contact information? Does their website copy have a certain tone, and does it talk directly to their target market (or does it focus on themselves)?
- Take a quick look at their social media feeds. What do you notice about each one? Do your competitors speak in a certain tone or use specific colors for their posts? Perhaps you notice their Instagram feed looks cluttered and busy—this could be an opportunity to position your brand differently.

The whole point of doing brand positioning is to figure out **how** you will communicate with your target. Now that you have some notes from your competitor research, you can come up with some ways to differentiate by asking yourself these questions:

- What do I like about the online presence of my competitors? What are they doing really well with their logos, social media, colors, and websites? (These are concepts you can also use, as long as you are very careful

not to plagiarize.)
- What do I dislike about the way my competitors show up online?
- What could I do differently from my competitors to stand out from them online?

Create Your Brand Positioning Statement

A **brand positioning statement** is a one- to two-sentence summary of your brand positioning. **Your brand positioning statement speaks to your target in a way your competitors don't.** It has to be unique, straightforward, and strong, so that it will be memorable and engaging. No matter the industry, every single business can stand out with a well-written statement. The main purpose of writing one is to completely separate yourself from the competition by strongly stating who you are, what you stand for, who your business serves, and how your target can benefit from investing in your product or service. All marketing and advertising efforts and tactics should be focused around the positioning statement as well. It is a powerful tool for businesses of all sizes.

The statement includes segmentation, targeting, and positioning. Basically, it needs to include your business name, the product or service itself, target audience, one main benefit, and a reason to believe.

There are a few different ways to create a brand positioning statement. To start and write one, you need to identify your target with one or two words. You can even use a few words such as "people who work from home," but the shorter the better—the more specific you are, the more powerful your statement will be. Your target can be engineers, writers, doctors, designers, etc. Your target doesn't have to be super small (niched), but try to identify a single group on which to focus.

Next, develop a list of needs these potential customers have. What would they like to have or do? Would they like to have an office space, a meeting room, a new decoration for their kitchen, or healthy snacks? Use that in your statement—be direct and specific. You need to make them feel like you are talking directly to them, like it's a one-to-one conversation.

Then, make a list of services or products you offer for that target—a list that helps them solve problems or addresses needs that they have. Choose one or two main offers and create one or two reasons why they should believe in you and invest in you.

Finally, you can put all of these pieces together to make your unique brand position statement. Your position statement will look something like this: (brand name) provides (service) to/for (target), because (reason) can (benefit).

You can also use: For (target), (brand name) provides (benefit) for people who (reason).

Feel free to be creative with these five segments. Resist the urge to add fluff words that don't mean much—the more direct your brand positioning statement is, the more effective it will be.

Here is an example from my coworking space that I mentioned earlier: "MELD Coworking provides shared office space for people who work from home so they don't feel lonely and are more productive." Or even more specific: "For entrepreneurs, MELD Coworking provides part-time memberships in a shared office space to make connections with other business owners and grow their network in Austin." You can always add the location. One more example: Nike's positioning statement is, "For serious athletes (target), Nike (brand name) gives confidence (benefit) that provides the perfect shoe (the product) for every sport".

You have control in positioning your business, so don't waste the opportunity to speak to your target audience in a way that will make them feel connected with your brand.

7 Brand Attributes & Voice

Do you know how a potential customer would describe your brand? Not you, your family, or your friends, but your customer. If someone didn't know anything about your business, would they say your brand is friendly? Boring? Different? Do you have any idea what they would say about your business at all?

People create their opinions of brands based on their previous experiences and on what they see, hear, and know. We have an opinion about McDonalds, we have some thoughts about Dolce & Gabbana, we know a lot about Apple, Samsung, Facebook, Pepsi, and Walmart, and this concept doesn't just apply to famous brands. We also have opinions on how a certain lamp looks in a store, what shirts we like or don't like, what vacuum to purchase, and what sparkling water we prefer. It's all based on something that we created thoughts about. It's either a) *we know what the brand is*, we know something about it, and we think about the brand based on the experience we had in the past, or b) *we don't know anything about the brand*, we create thoughts based on what we hear (from a family, friend, partner...) or simply based on what we saw in the moment.

It is completely the same when it comes to you and your brand. People will create their own opinions about your brand, whether you want them to or not. So help them create a good one!

Brand attributes are the characteristics that your audience sees as an inherent part of your brand. Even if you haven't yet mapped out a brand strategy and pinpointed your brand attributes, your brand already has natural attributes—it will just take a few strategic steps to identify them.

If you can be knowledgeable, organized, helpful, and friendly, your business can be as well. You just need to think of your business like it's a person first! And then later you can discover how that 'person' can talk to your target about himself without telling them directly who he is and what he stands for. It's similar to how you don't just approach a group of people and tell them you are friendly, helpful, organized, and knowledgeable. They create an opinion about you based on how you look, how you talk, and your behavior—or, in other words, your characteristics.

It's important to define your brand attributes before you start to think about visuals because your attributes are going to be translated into visuals. Your logo, business cards, flyers, and website will all depend on your brand attributes—whether your brand is serious or childish, luxury or affordable, simple or complex. It will be impossible for a graphic designer to design a good, successful logo if you can't communicate the personality of your business. Brand attributes will be reflected in the colors, shapes, language, social media, website, and overall feel of your brand.

There are a few different ways to create a list of attributes that can help your business communicate who it is, what it stands for, and why it's different. Notice that this is different from brand positioning as it is not focused on *separating* yourself from the competition, but rather it's how to *sound different* from the competition. If there are two different companies that offer similar coats, they will have different messaging, different ads, different videos, and they will *sound different.* One company can make us think it's a luxury brand, while the other can make us think it's a local small shop.

The simplest way to define your brand attributes is to pretend your brand is a person. Write down all the attributes of that person. For example, his name is Nick and he is friendly, smart, welcoming, successful, and professional.

Like Nick, Adidas is also seen as successful, smart, and professional. When consumers think of Tesla, they think of innovation. Starbucks evokes feelings of consistency and quality.

These are the "first impression values," which are the most important for people who have never heard about a specific brand before. People generate their first impressions not only based on their own perceptions, but also on what a brand has placed in front of them. These are characteristics that we might not know/think about yet, but we actually create the entire picture about the brand based on these characteristics.

We didn't just decide that Adidas sounds "smart." We think that based on what we have previously seen, heard, and learned about Adidas. The very first impression of IKEA is that it's an affordable, modern store whose furniture is designed for small spaces. IKEA is focused on families, it has a yellow and blue logo, and it's based in Sweden. This is what comes to mind when I think about IKEA, and that is how I would describe it—which is the most important: how a *customer* describes a brand.

Brand attributes are a combination of the culture of a brand, potential customers, emotions those customers have, and a brand voice. I will explain each of these four components, give you examples, and help you understand how to develop attributes for your business.

Culture	Customer / User	Voice	Emotions / Feelings
Smart	Organized	Friendly	Helped
Knowledgeable	Educated	Professional	Satisfied
Problem-solving	Confident	Positive	Relieved
Purposeful	Energetic	Clever	Strong

Brand Attributes: 4 Main Components and Examples

Brand culture is where that brand is coming from—it is the why. Why does IKEA create flexible and modular couches? Maybe the founder of IKEA couldn't find a couch that he liked and that would fit his small living room, so he decided to create one. Then he decided to start a business based on the solution he couldn't find for himself. So, that company would be clever, resourceful, driven, and problem-solving —exactly what the founder is.

For your own business, start by thinking about why you originally created it. Maybe you are selling essential oils. But why?

Brand Attributes & Voice

There are so many essential oil companies. Plus everyone can buy oils online, in grocery stores, in gift shops—everywhere. You need to find your why and set yourself apart. Even if it feels like you purely started for the money, take a moment to reflect on the deeper reason behind why you chose that specific industry. It doesn't have to be anything crazy. You don't have to go too deep into finding (or imagining) your why. Maybe you started your business because you had migraines and you previously tried everything, but nothing has helped you. You visited different doctors, tried so many different pills, tried to sleep more/less...until you found out that essential oils were the only thing that helped you. Then, you purchased some to try and they really worked for you, and now your company is all about providing education for people with the same problems you experienced. Now you know that oils are the solution, and you're not selling just essential oils to people—you are helping and educating them about the solution. The culture of your company in this case is: helpful, friendly, educational, nurturing, knowledgeable, smart.

Believe it or not, I started my branding studio simply because I couldn't find a job. Literally. I applied for so many different graphic design positions, but nothing was the right fit. I didn't know what to do—I was lost. Then I started freelancing because I thought that would help, but I couldn't find enough clients. It was so frustrating, but I was determined, and these obstacles only strengthened my desire to be successful. I was not making money, but I knew that one day I would—I just needed to figure it out. I was so focused on how to scale my business at the time, and I read every single article online about branding, marketing and advertising. Then I realized that just creating nice-looking marks as a graphic designer didn't help my clients scale their businesses, and I knew I had to make changes to my business in order to actually help them. I understood that my clients needed a plan and strategy for their business and brand, and I added additional brand strategy services to my business to help them connect with their target. Because I was so persistent and refused to give up, my brand's cultural attribute is: entrepreneurial-focused. The rest of my company's attributes are: helpful, resourceful, stress-free and organized.

If you try to describe your **potential customer**, how would you describe them? What would you say is your ideal client? Is he focused, clean, positive, objective? Here you need to find words to describe *whom you would want to work with*. So, not negative attributes, but only positive ones, only the ones that you will use in your branding. Even if you would say that your ideal client is unorganized (let's say you are a CPA), you would use the word *organized* so they feel organized when interacting with you and your brand.

When we talk about the **emotions** related to brand attributes, we focus on emotions your customers will have *after* using your product or service. Potential clients are going to use both their rational and emotional sides when making decisions. A rational approach might be, "I need to buy this and I have enough money." Emotions are just as important since that is usually the last decision-maker before purchasing.

Let's say you need to buy a mug. You have money for it, and you see two different mugs available. You will decide which one to buy based on your emotions and how you feel about each one. Here, we look for positive attributes only because that is how we want to make a customer feel. Once you bought your mug, you felt happy and satisfied. You felt good about investing in something you need and like, and you feel great overall. Now, you need to think about how you will make your customers feel after they interact with your company. These attributes will help you identify what your business needs to demonstrate even before your target reaches out to you.

So, if our customers are unhappy, we want to make them happy, or if they are insecure, we want to make them feel confident. If you are a photographer, most of your clients might come to you uncertain about how they are going to pose and unsure of what the end result will be. They might be insecure, skeptical, and maybe even worried. Your brand (in this case, you) therefore needs to be secure, professional, careful, and trustworthy. These attributes will help your potential clients feel connected and engaged with your brand. You need to make people feel relaxed but confident when working with you. You need to tell them if their makeup is messed up or the light is not good. Your job is to make them feel confident. Be *professional*!

Brand voice is how a business sounds to others. Besides messaging, your brand's voice describes how your logo, website, stationery, and other visuals will 'sound' to your audience. It is the merger of the attributes, messaging, and target research into a strategy—or voice—for visual and verbal communication. It can sound creative, friendly, exciting, or any number of ways—you just need to write down how you want your business to sound to people. Louis Vuitton's voice conveys luxury, high fashion, and contemporary style. All of their products communicate that as well.

Brand voice is the most important when it comes to visuals. These are the characteristics that will be used the most by a graphic designer working on your logo, business cards, and website. The design communicates these attributes, and when a consumer considers your business, they will know what your business attributes are. That is how your brand can build recognition and consistency in how it sounds to others.

A brand should speak with one voice on all platforms and mediums, including its website, flyers, social media, videos, etc. In order to keep a brand memorable, all elements need to be combined and your brand needs to appear the same everywhere so it can be recognizable.

A brand strategist would use these four steps (sometimes even more) when defining brand attributes. She wouldn't use all of them, and some of the steps would end up repeating anyway. She would choose **one attribute from each step, and those would be the brand's four main attributes!**

It's vital to make your brand intentional, identify its unique personality, and use the corresponding brand attributes to establish consistency and trust with your target market.

People will think whatever they want to think about your business. They will always have their opinion. So it's up to you to help them make an accurate judgment of your brand based on the content, visuals, and tone that you share with them. You will decide what they see first, and through your defined attributes you will describe your brand to the public. Therefore, your consumers will ultimately create their opinions based on what *you* present for *your brand*.

Your company can be whatever you want it to be. If you're unsure, your potential clients will be unsure too. It will be really hard to grow and scale your business without a clear picture of how you want your brand to look and sound. If you put yourself in your client's shoes, would you buy something you are not sure about? Would you be attracted to something you are not comfortable with? The answer is clearly no. So, how would someone describe your brand today?

8 Content Strategy

In the Target Profiles chapter, we talked about your target audience, your ideal customer, and your potential buyers. Knowing your target audience will help you determine your content strategy.

Content strategy is a process that includes planning, developing, and managing all of the content your business has (or should have). Content can include writing, photos, videos, or other media. **Getting the right content in front of the right people at the right time is what will make your business successful.** Through strategic planning you can have the right headlines, website copy, and social media posts so that people are attracted, connected, and engaged with your business. If you can accomplish that, your target audience will feel like you are communicating directly to them, and because they feel aligned with the message your brand expresses, they will want to learn more and eventually buy your services or product.

Your content plan is related to your brand positioning, brand attributes, and brand voice. As a reminder, your brand positioning helps you to know who your competitors are and how they interact with your target. Your content plan helps you figure out how to stand out, communicate differently, and which platforms to use when attracting your clients. Brand attributes are characteristics that describe your brand and your brand's personality. Based on those attributes, your brand will have a unique tone when creating content. You will need to know what your brand voice sounds like so you can consistently communicate with that voice. Do you need to sound serious, fun, educational, or friendly?

In order to start creating content for your business, you need to know all of the above.

At first, you might think that your business doesn't need a content strategy. I thought that too. I figured I would just create content as I went along. But as it turned out, I wasted so much time trying to figure out what was important for my customers to hear. I wasn't organized, and didn't have any strategy behind my actions, so I was always frustrated and lost in my own business, and that made it a challenge to create content. Can you relate?

After I developed a clear content strategy, which is what I'm going to teach you in the next few pages, I realized that content doesn't have to be so confusing. Imagine having a list of things you need to write about (or even if you hire a writer, you just give the list to them) and you never struggle trying to figure out what you need.

After I embraced the process and strategy behind creating content, I now always have a list of my next 20 blog posts. Each blog has a title and subtitles, and I even have notes for what kind of images I will need for each post. Now I actually feel excited about writing my next post, since I'm no longer overwhelmed by thinking, "Oh, I have to create content again..."

But why is your content important in the first place? Let's say you need a doctor, and you visit a few doctors' websites in order to find one. They all have professional websites, but only one of these doctors has reviews on their website, a blog with educational posts about different health topics, and a page that clearly says who they are and what they do. With the others, you are not sure what they do, they don't have a list of services, they don't have a doctor's biography, and they don't talk professionally about their specialties. Which doctor will you choose? The one that is positioning themselves as an expert by providing helpful articles on their website or the one that just says, "I am a doctor and I can help with this medical condition."

Your content doesn't have to be a blog. Your content might just be solid website copy, or maybe you send out a regular newsletter to people who sign up on your mailing list. Also, your content strategy will dictate the choice of images and videos and other media that resonates with the target. In this example, a doctor shouldn't have sick patients on his home page, but maybe the website could feature a healthy family, reflecting the way we want to feel after using his services—something that makes us feel confident. Now, think about your services or product. What would your customers like to hear, see, learn, and feel when they come across your website or social media pages?

Every aspect of your business involves your content strategy in some way. At the very beginning stages of your company, your content starts with a business plan, mission, and vision statement. Next it goes through the brand strategy, and it continues all the way to headers, taglines, and finally even your website structure itself, since your content and brand voice can dictate website design. Your website, flyers, and print or digital marketing materials will visually depend on how much, and what kind of, content you have. Your website might have two or five pages, based on how much content you have, how much your target needs to know about your company, and the nature of your business. The size and design of your flyers will depend on how much text you have and how many images you want to use. It's that simple.

Content strategy is also part of your marketing strategy. If your target is using social media platforms, you will want to make sure your content is showing up on those same platforms where they can see it. Isn't it easier to establish a few basic brand guidelines about what and when to post rather than trying to figure that out over and over again? On social media pages you need to be direct and offer a value that immediately resonates with your target. People do not have time to think about your posts, nor to read every word of them while scrolling on their phone, so your message needs to be short, clear, powerful, and consistent, with all the right keywords. Keywords are a group of words that are related to your business. Be sure to include your keywords in your videos, blog posts, social media posts, and other forms of communication to ensure that your content presents a unified message. My keywords are: branding, strategy, entrepreneurship, startup, business, and design.

A content strategy helps you determine which sentences sound right and which phrases your target reacts to. If you have a special sale or discount, you can plan what to say and where to say it in order to attract your potential consumers. Maybe you need to write educational articles and build an audience so that later you can offer them your services or products, and a pre-planned content strategy will help you be more efficient, structured, and organized.

For example, my potential clients might be looking for "website design," but they don't know that they need "brand strategy" first before designing a website. As we mentioned, you can have the best-looking website in the world, but if it doesn't convert your visitors into paying customers, why even have the website? Your website content is also important for search engine optimization (SEO) so that people can find your business in the first place, but we will talk more about that in Chapter 13: Designs for Your Business.

My blog and my posts are similar to this book. I educate my audience. I spend time to actually learn what their pain points are and how I can create the solution for them. They read about brand strategy over and over again. After a while, they either hire me for the services I offer or refer me to someone who needs my services because they know I can help them. By consistently providing the right kind of useful content, I built trust with my target audience.

It might seem overwhelming at first, but let me demonstrate how to simplify your content strategy, easily find topics, and create new content all the time.

Creating Your Content Plan

So, how do you create a content plan? Where do you start?

In the previous chapters, we went through the details of brand positioning and competitors, values, target profiles, and brand attributes. As mentioned, we will use all of these concepts when creating content strategy. You will need to know your brand values, who your target is, and what your core strengths are (compared to your competitors).

But first, you need to get extremely clear on the overall purpose of creating content for your business. Are you doing it just to have more content out there, just to put something on a website or in a book? No! When it comes to content strategy for your business, **the overarching goal of your content is always to lead to a purchase.** You need content for your website so that people can purchase what you offer, and you need content for social media so you can build brand awareness and eventually make people invest in your brand or business. To make it easier, you can break this process down into smaller goals: "I need to generate more leads (and then I will have more purchases)," "I need to attract past customers (so they will purchase something new)," or "I need better SEO (so people can find my business online, and then purchase from me)." You need to develop a plan for how your content will lead to people making an investment in your business.

Once you have your smaller goal in mind, you can think about what types of content will be the most attractive to your target customers. When we talk about content strategy in business, there are many different types of content you can choose from, including:

- Blog posts and other research articles
- Social media posts (You have a variety of social media platforms to choose from!)
- Pre-recorded videos
- Live videos
- Podcasts
- Infographics

Get into your ideal client's head and lifestyle for a minute. What formats of content do you think they prefer? Would they rather read a blog or watch a video? Do they like to listen to podcasts on their commute? Or do they prefer information presented visually, like in a graphic or infographic? Having this information will be an important part of your content strategy because you will need to create content for the right platform.

It's okay if you aren't 100% sure of your audience's content preferences because a large part of your content strategy will involve experimentation. Once you choose a few formats and begin creating valuable content for your target, you will be able to see which formats and topics are the most popular—and you can tweak your strategy from there.

Besides the goal and format of your content, it's important to think about the objective behind your content. Your objective will answer the question: Why are you making the content in the first place? Examples of objectives are to entertain, to educate, to inspire—a reason why people would engage and like your content. For example, in my branding company we write educational articles because a lot of entrepreneurs find them useful. Our objective is to educate, and because we have tailored our content to be educational, our target market keeps coming back to our articles to learn more,

After you determine your objective, you can start coming up with content ideas. The easiest way to do this is to develop your value proposition, and then use that value proposition to influence new content ideas. Your value proposition, or brand promise, is something specific that you promise to deliver to your customers. It's not just saying, "Hey, you will have an amazing website when I create it," but it's more like saying, "Hey, your website will have more qualified leads and a higher conversation rate when I create it." You need to focus on your client's problems and how you can solve those problems by promising you can do it and explaining how. So, what can you promise that people will get when they invest in your product or service? Try to be very specific here and speak to their tangible desires, because you need to include that one thing that they want to hear!

To develop your unique value proposition, summarize the following in one or two sentences:

- What is your company?
- How can your business solve your target's problems or improve their current situation?
- What specific value do you offer?
- Why should your ideal clients buy from you (and not from your competitors)?

Once you have completed your value proposition, you will use it on your landing page on your website, in your blogs, on your brochures, and so on.

The next step is to expand your content based on these ideas. You can't just use the same sentence or two over and over again. By using the unique value proposition that you just created, you can create a variety of brand stories.

Content Strategy

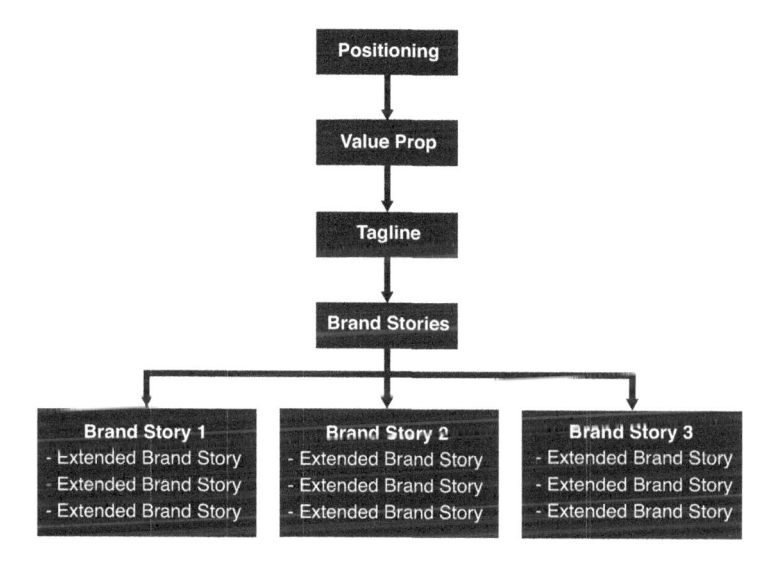

```
Positioning
    ↓
Value Prop
    ↓
Tagline
    ↓
Brand Stories
```

Brand Story 1	Brand Story 2	Brand Story 3
- Extended Brand Story	- Extended Brand Story	- Extended Brand Story
- Extended Brand Story	- Extended Brand Story	- Extended Brand Story
- Extended Brand Story	- Extended Brand Story	- Extended Brand Story

Brand stories are stories about your company, similar to taglines, that you can use and repeat depending on the platform. For example, a coffee company can use "daily brewed," "fresh beans," and "distinct flavors" as their three main brand stories. From there, they can expand into three more brand stories that branch from each one. So, "daily brewed" can be: "Every morning at 6 am, we freshly brew our coffee for customers who need a coffee to go." Then the next one can be: "Are you ready for our daily brewed cold brew?" Then: "Every day, we brew our coffee so it's always fresh." Once you do that with all your brand stories, you will have at least nine new sentences that you can expand into paragraphs, blog posts, flyers, or even a book.

To make sure your content matches what your target is seeking, you can create a keyword list based on your buyer persona's common search terms. Think about what they might look for before finding you. My target, for example, is searching for a logo design because most of them don't know that

93

they need brand strategy before developing a logo. So even though I focus on brand strategy, I write some content about logos in order for them to find me. What are your customers looking for? What do they *think* they need?

The most important thing is to make your content relevant to your target market and keep it consistent. That way, people will resonate with your business and remember you. They will use your product or services—and come back. You want them to feel satisfied and share their experiences with their friends and family, and these recommendations will help you scale your business.

All of your content needs to speak to *one person*. Yes, literally to "one person." Which sounds better: "We provide the best chairs for all of you," or "We provide the best chair for *you*." Your target needs to know that you are talking directly to them.

Content strategy, when done correctly, can be a powerful force that drives people to your business. If you don't do it right the first time, don't worry. It's easy to create new content as you go along, and with every piece of content you create, you will learn more about what does and (maybe even more importantly) doesn't work for your company. And even if your business shifts in another direction or you completely change your target, you can keep creating relevant content based on your new direction and customer base. Update your content as often as you need to. Some of your content strategy, like your keywords, will likely stay consistent—but the rest don't have to.

The final and crucial piece of your content strategy is to measure your results. You might create videos because you think your audience likes them, but then when you look at the website statistics, you discover that your audience actually prefers blog posts. There are different online tools to help you analyze your user feedback as well as how many reviews, views, comments, and other forms of engagement you have.

By reviewing analytic data, you will be able to see what your audience liked as well as what they didn't like. Use these metrics as a guide as you continue to create content. You can focus on the content topics and formats they prefer and continue to give them what they want.

9 Choosing the Right Branding for Your Business

Have you ever been confused over whether you should brand your business or brand yourself? Should you go by your company's name or by your personal name? How do you separate the two—or if you don't separate the two, how do you merge who you are with what your business is about?

If you are already in business, you might already be following the best strategy for you, but it's also possible that you're making a mistake and losing opportunities just by branding the wrong way.

When I started, I put everything into branding my company as KD Branding instead of branding myself as Kady Sandel. Since my business and services have drastically changed since then, I had to rebrand my company, including the name itself. So, the new name of my company—Aventive Studio—

was unknown, and my own name as a designer was also unknown because I had spent all of my energy on branding the company I didn't focus on anymore. If I had put everything into branding myself as Kady Sandel from the beginning, my company's name wouldn't have made that big of a difference for my clients, and I could have built continued name recognition. However, since my goal was to build a successful branding studio and make the studio well-known—and not to be a freelancer and well-known designer—this worked well in the end.

It is never too late to revamp your plans and start focusing on yourself or focusing on your business, so don't think this chapter is useless. Even if you already know that what you are doing is the right thing, this chapter might just confirm that you are right. But as one of my entrepreneur friends just realized after two years in business: her branding was wrong. She had focused on solely branding the business name, when really her customers were interested in her and her personal brand as well. Sometimes, what the market wants is not what we want, so it's always good to re-evaluate and make sure our current efforts still make sense.

Some professions and cases are obvious. If you're a coach or writer, for example, you would usually want to brand yourself, but if you were opening an IT company, you would want to brand the company. But most entrepreneurs struggle with this. It's not just about the name of your business; it's about the business's behavior and branding your business. Let me explain that through a well-known personal name and famous brand—Steve Jobs & Apple.

Steve Jobs built a brand around himself, and he also built a brand around his company. He had a personal brand. Apple had a professional brand. From there, they were able to market whatever products they were pushing at the moment: computers, iPhones, streaming services. But if they had skipped the important steps of branding Steve Jobs and Apple, and instead put all of their energy solely behind branding iPods, what would have happened to their company when people stopped using iPods?

It's not personal branding vs. corporate branding. **It's personal branding plus corporate branding.** You are the person who created your brand, and then your brand also has its own personality. Even if you have "just" a product, who is going to talk about that product more eloquently than you? Who could possibly be more passionate about your business and your brand than you? There is a huge difference between promoting a video with a professional speaker talking about your product, or a video where you are talking about why and how you started your company, what your vision is, and then what the product is. People will more likely resonate more with your personal story than they would connect with a salesperson talking about a random product.

However, this is not a hard-and-fast rule. Every strategy works at one point or another, but the real question is: What strategies will work for you and your company? From my personal experience, it's easier to get off the ground when the CEO or owner is the face of a brand or business, but you can always be in the background and just run the operational side, if that works for your business. There are a ton of companies that have owners we've never heard anything about. It worked for them and it might work for you too.

The key is connection. What resonates with your potential buyers? I understand that some small business owners don't want to be known as face of their company. Maybe they just want to make passive income. But guess what? People would still rather buy products from people they know, people who told their story and shared their vision, than from people they don't know anything about. Even if they only "meet" you online through videos or webinars, they still trust you more because you have made a connection with them.

Also, you might decide to start another company or launch a new product with a new name, but *your personal name* is always the same, so your personal branding will always stay with you. In the case of branding products, it will be easier if you make a brand around yourself and your company—and then push the product.

So which do you choose—a personal or corporate brand? There are pros and cons for each. On one hand, a personal brand may give you the status of an expert in your field, and you could scale that way, but on the other hand a corporate brand might help more with building trust with your audience and would look more professional.

There are many things you need to consider before deciding how you are going to proceed. The main one is: What are you selling? If you are offering services, you will most likely need to go by your personal brand but still maintain a company's name in case you decide to scale your business and start hiring. In the beginning, you will attend networking events, position yourself as an expert, act as a person with whom other people want to connect, and be the one who is building relationships.

Even when you're selling a product, you are still the one who is talking to the audience. A friend and fellow entrepreneur and small business owner said to me recently, "You know what I realized? I have a product, and as much as I hate being in front of the camera and not wanting to be the face of my company, I have to. My product on its own doesn't connect to my people as much as it does when they see me talking about the product. One day, I will have the flexibility, but right now, I have to focus on building my personal brand in order to build my business's brand." Create a brand around yourself, be willing to change directions if your current efforts aren't working, and the rest will follow.

Everything depends on the type of a business you have, so if you are opening a local restaurant, you are most likely going to brand your business around the location and the business itself and not around you. Your customers don't care much about who the owner is, but they do care about the customer service, ambience, food, drinks, etc.

You can always test it and do a little bit of both and see how that goes. See what works better for you and your target. Once you see that one strategy is working over another, just stick with that one and push as much as you can, and you will see the success you are looking for.

Branding Products vs. Branding Services

Branding for products is very similar to branding for services, and in some cases the strategies are the same. The main difference is that when you brand a product, the focus is on the visuals, presentation, and feeling, while with services it's all about the story, the examples, and potential results. Also keep in mind there is a difference between *selling* a product or services vs. *branding* a product or services.

Let's talk about selling first. If you have a product, then you already know exactly what you are selling, what it is, and how much it costs—and even more importantly, your customers know that as well. A good product is typically easier to sell than a good service. Of course, it's not all black and white. If you don't have the right brand strategy, attractive design, and the right marketing plan, nothing will work even if you have the best product in the world. But in this comparison, selling a product is easier because people can see a product, while it's harder for them to imagine the end result of your services. If a person sees shoes on a shelf, and those are the shoes he was looking for, he will buy them.

Having a product means that you put a lot of time into advertising, marketing, talking about the product, and showing the product. From there, people either resonate and buy it, or they don't. But when you're selling services, you are basically selling your time based on something. That "something" is usually your knowledge, your previous experience, your skill, or what you will provide in a certain time frame.

Selling your time for money can work really well for coaches, therapists, massage therapists, and pet-sitters, but it doesn't work for all service providers, and there is a small problem with this type of pricing structure. As a designer, the more experience I have, the faster I can get the work done. Does that mean I should make less money now because I spend less time working than someone with less experience? Even if my hourly rate goes up, there is only a certain amount that people will pay for hourly services, so this model just doesn't work. Instead, I always charge per project so I get paid based on how much value I provide. If my design helps you make $10,000, you can pay me $1,000, right? And if I help you make $100,000, you should pay me $10,000 because you just made $90,000 because of me. As mentioned, this is not for everyone either, but if you can find a way to get paid for the **value you provide**, you will make more money and people will appreciate you more because you're providing the results they care about.

When your pricing is determined by the value you provide, you are "packaging" your services as a product. This might not work for certain professions (such as lawyers, writers, or therapists), but it can work really well for designers, developers, or photographers.

Now that we've covered selling your products or services, let's refocus on branding. When branding your services, you need to make a strong connection with a potential buyer. They need to trust you more than if you had a product. Your customers don't physically see what they are buying, so they need to resonate with the story you share with them. They need to meet you on a deeper level—to understand why, how and what your offering is, and what benefits they are getting. While working on your brand strategy, keep in mind that your audience needs to build a deeper relationship with you and trust in your ability to deliver results.

On the other hand, if your business has products, your main focus will be on visuals and how those visuals make people feel. Branding for products can be a little bit easier than branding for services because people understand the results—they physically see what items they will receive. You can always support your product by talking about your brand, sharing articles, and educating them, but your main focus is on what people see. So if you are branding a product, make sure that your visual design is a top priority.

Online or Offline?

People like to argue about whether online or offline branding (and marketing and advertising) is more important. While the whole world is online and branding efforts tend to lean in that direction, there are still in-person networking events that you can attend in order to meet new people, build relationships, collaborate, and generate new business connections. Some businesses are exclusively online, and that's fine if you have well-developed branding and a solid online marketing strategy. Online human connection is harder to develop than meeting people in person. So, yes, it depends on the business, which leads us to look back at who our target is and where they hang out.

This process will vary slightly depending on whether you offer services or products. Products are most likely going to be sold online, while service providers can build stronger relationships in person. However, I think that networking events can help everyone—even businesses with online products. You can always meet someone who has similar products, challenges, or solutions to yours, and you can gain knowledge. Maybe that one person you meet at a cocktail hour will help you set up your website or suggest a new marketing idea that changes everything for your company.

But to be clear: Don't ever go to a networking event hoping to sell. Go to meet people and build your network—that's why it's called "networking." When I was starting and people told me, "Networking is a giver's game." I was like, "Yeah, but *I need* more business." It took me awhile to realize that as you send more referrals to someone, they will want to give back by sending referrals back to you.

I had to learn how to network. Networking seems easy at first, like you just go to an event, talk with someone, say what you do, they say what they do, exchange business cards, and that's it. Except it doesn't really work that way.

First you need to know what your "things to listen for" are. For example, when I go to networking events, I listen for people who say, "I'm starting a company" or "I would like to grow my business," but not, "I'm looking for a brand strategist" even though brand strategy is what I offer. Remember: Your future clients don't use your words.

Once you're clear on what your clients are looking for, find events where you can meet people who have the same target audience as you. The people you meet at these events can be your referral partners. As a designer, my referral partners include commercial brokers, investors, and small B2B companies such as marketing and advertising agencies.

Once you connect with your referral partners, tell them what phrases you're listening for. Every time they hear people mention those key phrases, they will think of you. However, you still need their business card so you can send a follow-up email. If you think you can help your new connections by introducing them to other people in your network, make those introductions. Your new referral partners will appreciate that, plus the other person will like that too. You can also set up a one-on-one meeting with your potential referral partner. This is where I find the most value. In these personal meetings that I set up after networking events, I get to know more about my new connections and the businesses they have, and I can share more about myself and what I'm looking for.

The point is to build relationships. Even if in-person networking is not what you would prefer for your business or you don't see much value in it, you still need to create connections and build relationships with people. The only difference is whether you build those relationships through conversations online (like email marketing) or conversations in person. In your messaging, whether it's online or offline, make sure to be consistent and speak directly to your target in a language they can understand.

If you can find a way to connect with people online and you simply don't feel like going to an event, do that. Some people are introverts and they put more effort into their online strategy. While it's harder to start a conversation with someone online than with a person who is standing right next to you, for some people online interaction works for them. They create a ton of content, they put that content everywhere via social media, blogs, and videos, and they connect with their clients and referral partners through these online platforms.

Do whatever feels more natural and comfortable to you, and more importantly, do what your target wants you to do. If you think that your ideal client is at a networking event or can find you through knowing people from networking events, go to the events. But if your ideal target works from home, for example, and is a freelancer, just be online.

10 Visual Branding

Most business owners think that visual branding is the most important part of branding. Some actually think that visual branding is branding. A lot of people make the mistake of going straight into visuals because they have never even heard about brand strategy I get inquiries such as "how much do you charge for logo design?" all the time. But how can I design a logo if I don't know for whom I am designing it? Even if I already know the company, if they haven't developed a brand strategy, then I don't know who their target is. Remember, we are never creating visuals for ourselves, but for our target market. The purpose of logos and other visual elements is to attract potential buyers, not us.

An important distinction here is the difference between visual identity and visual branding. **Your visual identity consists of design elements such as colors, materials, shapes,**

fonts (typography), and functionality. This is not the same as branding. Branding includes all the elements a company has, such as brand awareness, user profiles, videos, social media posts, logos, and content strategy—literally everything. A strong visual identity creates an emotional connection between the brand and consumer while also communicating the brand's values and personality through colors, shapes, and fonts. Successful visual branding creates a memorable experience for the consumer, makes them trust the company and feel safe, and encourages referrals and repeating business if the experience was great. Visual branding is one of the best tools you have to communicate with your customers, and it will be the most visible on your logo design, website, printed materials, videos, and other media.

Visual branding has a deeper purpose than just looking nice. It will help attract your ideal clients, explain what your company is about, show the value of your business, and use the right brand voice in order to resonate with your buyers. Your visual branding provides the first impression your potential customers have of your brand, which makes it extremely important. Therefore, your visuals should speak directly to your target, resonate with them, and make them want to learn more about you. Even if you have impeccable messaging, visuals are still the most effective way to c*apture your audience's attention* as visuals help build brand awareness and brand recognition.

I'm going to mention this one more time because it's so important: Without completing your brand strategy, I would not recommend working on visuals. If you already have a logo and website, complete your strategy first and then see if your existing visual identity fits with your new strategy. If you think you have to rebrand, that's okay—it's nothing to be afraid of.

Better now than later. But if you're just starting out, it's ideal to build a strong foundation now since rebranding can take a lot of time, effort, and money later.

Before developing its graphic designs, a business needs to have clear brand and design goals. There is no way a brand can have an amazing logo, proper business cards, a website that speaks to their target, and the right messaging if there's no brand strategy. I can have an amazing octopus illustration as a logo for my branding company, but why? How is that octopus going to position me a professional brand strategist and designer? How is that going to portray my business as a serious and professional company that works with business owners? It probably won't.

Furthermore, before you design a flyer or a website, you need to know how much content you'll have. If an entrepreneur doesn't know anything about content strategy and needs to write copy for his website, how would he do it—just write random things down, stick in some images, and say it's done? Or if a designer needs to design a logo for someone and doesn't know whether that business needs to "sound" serious, childish, luxurious, or affordable, how would she know what kind of logo to design?

Your visual branding is a reflection of your company, so before you develop your visuals, you will need a clearly defined strategy that identifies your target audience and your business goals. Yes, you will spend some time creating this strategy and developing all the pieces, but this is something that will actually save you time and money in the long run.

Poor visual branding can actually hurt your business.
People create assumptions around your brand based on what

they see. If they see something that looks childish, but your company should be serious and professional—they will think your company is childish. When you see Apple's logo, you don't think it's a kid's store. Your visual brand needs to precisely reflect your company's values, promises, personality, and purpose.

Visual branding needs to be attractive. People need to be attracted to your brand. The very first thing they see will be your logo, name, maybe a business card or a website. If your visual branding looks outdated, doesn't provide enough information, or doesn't click with a potential client, that client won't be interested enough to contact you for your services or try your product. Your visual identity needs to be something that wakes up the curiosity in them so they want to learn more. So here we are, going back to who your ideal client is. You need to design everything for that person.

Visual branding needs to be consistent. Brands that are consistent with their visual identity and branding resonate more effectively with their audience. All of the visual branding elements need to fit together, and they should be used over and over again on all the platforms your business is going to use. For example, you simply cannot have a billboard, business card, or website without your logo on it—your logo needs to be everywhere. Your visual elements should have the same (or similar) look and feel and messaging as well.

If you look at well-known branding such as Starbucks, you will notice that they always use their signature green color with their mermaid. They might have seasonal cups and mugs and use other colors, but they will always use the mermaid and/or their green color. Apple always uses white, black, and shades of gray. Coca-Cola? Always red and white.

Make sure you're using the same colors all the time—not similar colors, but *exactly the same*, in order for people to remember your brand through a consistent visual identity.

Such consistency is a huge part of visual branding because it helps people remember your business and keep coming back. Consistency builds trust since it creates a relationship. People can connect to your business once it becomes familiar—they will know how your brand feels, looks, and what the message is. The more consistent your messaging is, the easier it will be to build brand awareness and develop loyalty with customers.

Visual branding needs to be unique. In order to attract potential clients, your visuals need to be different and stand out. Do you remember what we talked about in the brand positioning chapter? You need to differentiate your business from similar businesses. Observe your competitors, see how their branding looks, and try to make your brand look different. Don't do this for the sake of being different (that's not always good!), but try to make yours look better, try to be unique and creative so people can remember your brand over the others that are in the same industry.

The key here is to not give potential customers a reason to leave. You want your potential clients to notice you because you stand out from all other brands. For example, everyone in the health industry is using blue, green, and white—healthy and trustful colors—and that's fine (we will talk about the psychology of colors in Chapter 12: Psychology as Universal Communication.) But if all of these health companies use similar logos, similar taglines, and the same purchased stock images, how would a customer choose one over another? I'm not saying that a hospital should have a pink logo, but that hospital could use shapes or imagery that other hospitals don't, but still keep its branding industry-appropriate.

Visual branding needs to be memorable. People need to remember your brand. There are so many similar businesses, and if your visual brand looks just like the rest, people will not remember your company, even if they already used your services or product!

How many times have you gone to a coffee shop, but you couldn't remember the name of it afterward? Maybe the logo had a coffee cup in it, just like all the others. You might have even tried to give a recommendation to your friend about the great latte you had four months ago when you were there, but you simply can't remember the name, and even when you Google it, all the coffee shops look the same. That business owner is missing an opportunity to get a new customer and scale their business.

Your potential clients need to remember your name, logo, colors, and shapes in order to return or recommend you to someone. If you had a client in the past and he needs you again, but he can't remember you, he is going to look for a similar business to buy from instead. Also, if he doesn't remember where to go back and find you, he can't give referrals to other people. He can't recommend your company to his friends and family if he simply doesn't remember you. You are clearly going to have a difficult time scaling your business if no one remembers you, so you need to find ways to stand out and create something different in order to be memorable.

Emotions. Emotions. Emotions. Keep this in mind all the time. People resonate and connect with brands based on their emotions, based on what they feel. When consumers think about how they like a certain shape or color, they feel enjoyment, happiness, trust. People are emotionally connected to people, places, objects, and brands. Your visual brand can tell a story and can be designed to create an emotional reaction that will lead your customers to interact with you. You can increase your sales just based on your visuals.

11 Brand Boards and Guidelines

A brand board is a short and easy-to-read document that includes all the *visual elements* of a brand. In order to keep your brand consistent and recognizable, this is one of the most important documents a business can have.

The main elements of visual branding are logo design, typography and fonts, color palette or color scheme, texture and patterns, photos and images. This is what's included in a brand board that every serious business needs to have.

A brand board is a road map of your brand with instructions on how to implement each brand element. Your brand board is a reference guide that can and should be shared with your printer, web designer, developers, and anyone who is working on your business's branding. It will ensure your logos, fonts, colors, and patterns remain consistent. Even if your marketing executive goes on vacation, or your web developer hires a subcontractor, or a new staff member needs to create slides for a presentation, your brand board will be available as a record of the visual elements of your brand.

Variations of a logo are extremely important because nowadays we have so many different platforms and formats where a business logo can be implemented. Ideally, every logo should have a horizontal (rectangle) and vertical (square) version. A company should always have one primary logo that represents them, but a secondary logo helps in situations where the primary cannot fit nicely. If your main logo is horizontal, but your company needs a version of the logo that can fit on its social media profiles (squares), a secondary logo is helpful.

Your brand can also create an icon from your logo, which can be useful but isn't necessary. That icon is called a logo submark. It's usually derived from your primary logo, and it can be initials, a monogram, or a small image. Logo submarks are often used as watermarks, favicons, parts of patterns, or Instagram Highlight covers.

Brand colors are included in your brand board so that you and everyone in your company can use the exact same colors on all your visual brand elements.

Usually, your company's brand will have two or three primary colors followed by three to five secondary colors (which are often shades of grey, white, or black). In the brand board document, a designer will include a hex code for each color to ensure the correct shades of your brand's colors will always be used in your logo, business cards, and website.

Typography is essential when it comes to your brand's consistency. Most of the time, a brand should only have two fonts but never more than three.

One of those fonts is the primary font used for stationery, flyers, and posters. The secondary font would go along with the primary font and would be used only for parts of text that need some accents. For example, sans serif fonts are clear enough to serve as your primary font, but hand-written fonts work better as secondary fonts. In certain cases, companies may opt to have a third font for website purposes only.

Texture & Patterns can help a lot when expressing the personality of a brand. Textures and patterns in your brand can be really complex or really simple, and they can be used to layer over your fonts or photography, or in other elements of your website. Examples of patterns used in branding include repeatable shapes and glittery texture. Do not use more than one pattern. Two or more can make your brand look like a few different brands, especially if the textures are not similar either in shapes, patterns, or colors.

A brand board section of **styled imagery** that includes sample stock photos can help your brand stay consistent, especially in your marketing materials and social media content. When you use the same style of images in your blog, social media, and email templates, you can increase brand awareness of your company.

Brand boards are important because the elements included on the brand board will keep the brand consistent and recognizable. Coca-Cola always has the same typography, and I'm sure you can even picture it now in your head just thinking about Coca-Cola. They also always have the same red color, the same image style (family, Christmas tree, etc.). They keep their brand consistent and recognizable.

If I go to your website and see that everything is blue, and then I go to your Instagram and everything is yellow, and then I see your business card is brown, I wouldn't be confident that all of these materials belonged to the same company or brand. I would think the inconsistency seemed weird, and I likely wouldn't trust your brand. I'm sure you wouldn't purposely use that extreme of colors, but even using light pink and bright pink interchangeably can confuse users. Basically, you want to avoid anything that could make users wonder if your brand is your brand or someone else's brand. When you see an Apple product, you don't think twice and wonder if Apple made it—the branding is so consistent that you just know. You want users to have the same experience with your brand: When they see your colors, fonts, and images, they immediately make an association with your company.

And not just that. If you are a blogger or any other solopreneur (individual) and need to create promotional materials such as newsletters or flyers, looking at your brand board can help you choose the best images, fonts, and colors. Brand boards actually save time because you don't need to look for what kind of content to incorporate and what colors to use—it's already outlined in your brand board! When you already have those pieces of your brand defined, you can focus on other spheres of your business.

Brand boards guide and dictate the whole brand. You or a designer will create a brand board at the same time as your logo, and definitely before your business cards, letterheads, brochures, website, and other visual elements of your brand. Sometimes you might even create your brand board before the logo, and then your designer can fit the logo into the brand board later. If you don't have a brand board, but you already have business cards, a website, or other branded items, that is okay, but you skipped a very important step. If that's the case for your business, I would highly recommend creating a brand board now that can guide your visual identity in the future. You can also work with a professional designer who will help you organize everything.

Having a brand board is a great way for you to implement all of your brand attributes. Your brand can feel warm and welcoming, or serious and bold, and this is how the colors, pictures, logo, and fonts should look. Once you have everything together in one board, compare your new brand board to your list of brand attributes and double-check that your brand board accurately reflects your business.

One note: Brand boards are not the same as **brand guidelines**. Brand boards are documents that show how your brand looks and what visual elements you should be using, while **brand guidelines are rules on how to use your brand.** Your brand guideline document will include different sizes for a logo, how much spacing a logo should have around it, what backgrounds your logo can have, what you can and cannot do with your logo (including stretching it), and other rules related to your visual identity. There are a lot of rules in a brand guideline document. Brand guides are pretty complex, and not all businesses need them, but either way, it is important to know how to use your designs.

In short, a brand board is a quick visual aid to promote consistency in making brand selections and decisions, whereas a brand guideline document is a much more in-depth 'rule book' that is important as your company scales. Think of it as a quick start guide (the brand board) versus a user manual (the brand guidelines); both are valuable and used in different contexts.

Before you create a brand board for your own business, you might research other companies (and your competitors). Document their websites, their social media banners, their fonts, and some of the images that they use. That will give you a feel for how they define their visual branding.

To start creating your brand board, choose two or three main colors. Those colors are your primary colors that you will use on all of your branding materials, such as your logo, business cards, and website. You need to have hex codes for those colors, which you can find by searching online for "Color Hex." There are a few websites that can guide you through this simple process. You will also need secondary colors, which complement the primary colors but will not be as heavily used as the main colors. Usually you will only need one secondary color or shades of black, white, and gray.

After that, you will need some fonts. I would suggest having one main font and one secondary font. For example, you might choose one serif (traditional style) or sans serif (contemporary) and one that is a display or handwriting font. The reason for the second font is not simply decorative or for design purposes but for accent purposes. Have you ever seen a company's logo in one font, and then their slogan is written in a second font? That way your words will stand out without blending into one another.

Once you have your fonts and color choices, explore a few different websites with images and download three to five (or even more) images that fit your brand attributes and your brand personality. In the future, every time when you want to use some images for your blog, flyer, or other materials, make sure that the photos and images you choose match the style of the photos you previously saved. That way you are developing brand consistency, which is the whole point of having a brand board in the first place.

Now that you've set your branding "feel" you are ready to start producing content for your brand. Refer to your branding board as often as you need to remind yourself of the unique look and feel of your brand. And remember: You should use only those colors, only those fonts, and *everything* you post—a blog, a photo, a layout of your text, truly everything—needs to match the brand board you just created.

I would not suggest creating a random brand board just to have it. Take the time to create one that will really fit your brand strategy in order to speak to your ideal client and attract potential buyers. Don't focus on what colors and fonts you like, but think about what would catch the eye of your customers. In the next chapter, we will talk a little bit about psychology and how people perceive different objects, shapes, and images, which will help you as well.

To see an example of a real brand board, visit www.aventivestudio.com/brand-board.

12 Psychology as Universal Communication

How on earth is psychology related to branding, and why do you need to know about the psychology of colors, shapes, and design? It's quite simple. **Because of the way our brains work, people perceive colors and shapes in certain and predictable ways.** Bright red doesn't make us as calm as light green can, for example. If you look at yoga studios, they use certain branding colors to make people feel relaxed, serene, and peaceful. I would bet that your local yoga studio uses significantly different branding elements than your local boxing gym because each business is different and has a different target.

Design does not just involve creating inspirational art, but also knowing how people will react to it. Design is a universal communication, which means that everyone in the world who sees the design should understand it. I don't mean that we should all speak the same language and be able to read content on every single website, but we all are attracted (or not attracted) to certain visual designs on a psychological level. Everyone in the world needs to *feel* the same when looking at one design.

There are universal psychological principles that a professional designer should follow. For example, gold is always perceived as a luxury color. Each color has its own meaning, and if you have a happy brand then you should use happy colors. We simply know what happy colors are because our brain reacts positively to certain colors and makes us feel happy. So if your brand attributes include the concepts *welcoming, happy*, and *open*, you shouldn't use colors like dark brown, gold, or black in your logo, website, or other design pieces.

Our brains also respond to certain shapes. A square is not as friendly as a circle because a circle is more "touchable"—something that people can use without thinking that they can hurt themselves, as opposed to a square and its angles. These are things that we don't actively think about when looking at designs, but our brain does. Rounding out a corner or moving some pieces inside a design can potentially change the entire meaning of that design.

Neither you nor your designer need to have a Ph.D. in psychology. All you need to do is understand the basics. In this short chapter, I will tell you a little bit about colors, shapes, and placement—just enough for you to feel comfortable with adjusting your brand or improving it.

As I mentioned, different **colors** have different meanings. What color do you think of when you hear the word "money"? How about "love"? One is a noun (object); one is a verb (feeling). For both words we have certain specific colors that pop into our minds. If you want people to think about money or love when they see or interact with your company, you should consider using shades of green or red, respectively, to make that connection in their minds. Colors usually have several different meanings or associations in color psychology. For example, green doesn't always indicate money, but that specific shade of green does. If you use bright or light green in your branding, you might create the feelings of "fresh," "healthy," and "new."

Both of my companies use blue in their visual identities. The coworking space that I own has some medium light blue in its logo and website, while my branding studio has a little bit more dark and bright blue.

Blue is often associated with depth and stability. Blue symbolizes trust, loyalty, wisdom, confidence, and intelligence. But there is a difference in shades as well. Light blue is associated with health (work from home is not always healthy, people need human interaction), understanding (working with like-minded people), tranquility (it's a workspace), and softness (having comfortable furniture and space to work from). Dark blue represents knowledge, power, integrity, and seriousness—which is perfect for my branding company.

Think about the brand attributes you previously defined. What colors would represent these attributes, and why? Remember: Don't use colors just because you personally like them. The colors you like might not be the colors that will attract your ideal clients, and those colors might not fit the personality of your brand or what your brand needs to be in order to succeed. Below you can find some examples of colors and their meanings.

- **Red:** energetic, active, passionate, powerful, strong, determined
- **Green:** growing, calm, natural, adaptable, relaxed, stable, harmonious, balanced
- **Blue:** loyal, trustworthy, reliable, responsible, authoritative, peaceful, idealistic
- **Yellow:** optimistic, enthusiastic, fun, creative, challenging, logical
- **Orange:** sociable, optimistic, independent, adventurous, informal, cheerful
- **Pink:** romantic, loving, understanding, sweet, feminine, intuitive, hopeful, warm
- **Brown:** down-to-earth, approachable, protective, strong, honest, quality, structured, stable, friendly
- **Gold:** successful, worthy, positive, optimistic, loving, wise, luxurious, charismatic
- **Purple:** creative, selfless, humanitarian, mysterious, fantastic, futuristic, inventive, unlimited
- **Gray:** reliable, neutral, mature, intelligent, classic, solid, stable, calming, elegant, formal, dependable
- **White:** clean, complete, simple, equal, open, new, neat
- **Black:** strong, protective, formal, sophisticated, comfortable, contained

What colors best represent your business? You could Google the color psychology of the ones you pick to learn more in-depth information about each one and make sure it's the right fit for your brand.

Shapes have their own meanings as well. Shapes can show customers a lot about your business, and the shapes you use will reflect if your business is artistic, friendly, or powerful. Just like colors, shapes speak to customers. Each shape has its own meaning and influences our mind and reactions differently.

What shape do you think of when you hear the word "building"? I assume it's a square or rectangle, and not a circle. Squares, rectangles, and triangles are the most-used shapes and we see them around us all the time. Our computers and monitors, cellphones, books, furniture, doors, and so on use square and rectangular shapes. Straight lines and angles give a sense of trust, security, reliability, and seriousness. Now, if your business has these attributes, your logo and other design elements will have more squares than round shapes. It's that easy. Circles, on the other hand, are more related to the sun, the earth, planets, rings, etc. They usually represent ideas of completion, wholeness, and harmony. Circles are also more feminine than masculine (squares) and can suggest movement. Think about balls, wheels, and watches. If your business is selling a lotion for women, your designs will most likely be closer to circular ones than squares and triangles.

Your task is to picture your ideal client and imagine what would attract them more: something soft, round, gentle, and smooth, or something strong, manly, rough, and firm. Your logo, website, flyers, and other visual elements should reflect that feeling as well. Your designs should have either soft or strong edges and loud or quiet (big or small) circles or squares (shapes).

Psychology of **placement** is a little bit more complicated, but once you know what it's about and how it works, it can be as easy as selecting colors or shades. Placement is related to what a human eye catches first. Let's talk about websites as an example. When someone lands on your home page, they need to know what to do next. If you scatter a lot of images, texts, and call-to-action buttons randomly on your website, your conversion rate will be lower because human eyes would just scan the website and maybe even completely overlook the buttons you want them to click. Your designs need to grab the consumer's attention. Everything needs to be well-designed with logical placement. Professional website designers actually make sketches (wireframes) in black and white, only using geometric shapes and lines to make a template. This process is just about placement and deciding where to put a photo, text, or header.

Shapes

Placements

Placement is important because people will only see and focus on one thing at a time. Attention spans are short in the online world, so it's up to you to decide what your potential buyers see first, what they see next, and how they can easily take the next step—whether that is buying your product, adding themselves to your email list, or some other action. If you are a clothing designer, you would want images of your designs to be seen first in order to attract your target, then a header of what you offer—what kind of clothing—followed by a page or a button with "see more." After that, you would add all the details and pricing. If you are a business coach, people don't care about your images as much, and you would want your header and subheader to be seen first so people can read why you are different and why they should choose you. Think about whether your business is primarily visual (like clothing and fashion design) or textual (like coaching, consulting, and writing). What do people need to see, and in what order?

Colors, shapes, and placements are not something you need to study or know in-depth, and I covered enough in this chapter for a small company, startup, or individual entrepreneur. Yes, colors, shapes, and placements will help with your business and brand, and they will affect how your brand is perceived by your audience, but don't spend too much time getting caught up in these aspects of branding. Think about the basics only. Just take a few moments to look at your target, your brand attributes, your competitors (what do they use?), and your goals, and make sure the colors and shapes you're using in your branding align with these concepts. If you desire further assistance when it comes to the psychology of design, you can consult with a designer who understands these concepts in greater depth.

13 Designs for Your Business

To gain proper recognition and trust, you need to develop some visual identity elements for your business. Not every business needs a flyer design, an envelope design, or a stamp design, but based on your brand strategy you can decide what designs your business needs and consult with a designer to create those materials. In this chapter, I will go through some of the "must have" elements—such as a logo and website—and what is important to consider in the design process.

But before I start, I would like to remind you about your target (again): Keep in mind that you are not designing the logo, website, or business cards for yourself, so it doesn't matter what you like. It's all about what attracts, communicates with, and connects with your potential customers because they are the ones who will buy your offering and help you grow your business.

Logo Design—*The face of your company*

Logo design is the visual centerpiece of a company. It gives your business an identity, sets your brand apart, and provides a foundation to build visual consistency and positive association. A well-designed logo provides recognition, communicates professionalism, and builds trust.

When designing or commissioning the design of a logo, you want to create something that is unique. Avoid templates and online logo purchases, particularly cheap resellers that are not transparent about (or they misrepresent) their sources or design process. You might not be able to register to protect your 'property' if someone else already uses the same mark. **Applications for trademarks that are too similar to existing registrations will be denied.** Furthermore, if someone else already registered it, you may be using yours illegally.

A logo should be designed in certain **vector-based programs** (such as Adobe Illustrator) in order to be scaled and printed without losing quality. Vector files are considered the original files. While various platforms require different formats (such as .ai, .pdf, .jpg, or .png) and resolutions, it is critical that you ask for and save the originals and not just the commonly exported formats.

Purchase the fonts that you plan to use so you have a license to use them. Note that font licenses can be for either personal or commercial use. A designer needs to use commercially licensed fonts.

Also, make sure you obtain a **license for your *own logo*.** Even though it's created with your business in mind, the designer created it and maintains all rights to use it as they wish unless rights are explicitly agreed to and transferred to your entity.

There are a lot of best practices and rules that a competent designer should be aware of, so if you don't have a design background, I highly recommend working with a designer rather than trying to DIY your logo. Sometimes overlooked is that a logo must be functional in **black and white** as well as in color (there are still a variety of mediums where you may desire a two-tone output). Other best practices include avoiding excessive detail, too many colors, mixing fonts, etc.

In summary, professional designers conduct research, apply your brand's voice, complete iterative sketches and creative experimentation, build vector-based designs, openly offer originals and the rights to designs, and they leverage licensed fonts and resources to design your logo.

Stationery—*Business correspondence*

Stationery typically includes business cards, letterhead, and envelopes. These are the most common forms of physical business correspondence and are early contributors to brand perception among your customers.

All these formats should feature your logo, brand colors, fonts, and relevant contact information, including your name, title, phone number, email address, website address, and physical address of your business (if applicable).

Besides the design elements defined by your brand board, there is printing-specific knowledge that's necessary to implement into your stationery designs. If the artwork touches the edges of a design, such as the border of a business card, it needs to incorporate **bleed**. Bleed is a printing term and ensures that no gaps at the edges occur in the final trimmed document.

Email signatures and other digital templates (i.e., Microsoft Office templates) should adopt the same design elements too.

In the end, all communication materials should consistently feature the characteristics defined by your brand strategy and, in turn, your brand board specifics.

Website— *The 24/7 portal to your brand*

A website that aligns with your company's branding, content strategy, and voice can expand the quality of your reach, build brand trust and awareness, and increase your revenue.

Every aspect of your company's website is important, but just like your strategy is the foundation to your brand, the platform on which you build your website is the foundation. The platform—backend of your website—is vitally important and will have a huge impact on what can be done and how it can be used. Consult with your web developer about choosing the right platform for your business model. Some are specifically built for selling products, some are for blogs, some are for portals, etc. Choosing the platform for your website is extremely important because if you make a mistake, you will need to rebuild the whole website.

Your website's functionality requirements depend on your business model and your target.

Your website can have one of these three goals: to provide information, to sell a product, or to make visitors contact you for your services. Choose your primary goal before developing the website.

Websites need to be attractive, engaging, easy to use, and responsive to all devices and browsers. When a visitor lands on your website and cannot easily find what they're looking for, they'll leave the website (this is referred to as the 'bounce rate'), and you'll lose a potential client. While most people recognize the importance of a well-designed and striking website, you should also view your website as a tool to grow your business. Therefore, you must also consider function and strategy relative to content, engagement, number and types of pages, user interface, and much more.

Your domain name and hosting speed are incredibly important. A domain name—your website address—is what a user needs to remember to find your site. Hosting speed is frequently underappreciated. A user's patience to stay on a website while it loads is fewer than 3 seconds. Their attention span isn't much better once they are on your site. In general, people stay about 5 seconds, so that's how much time you have to get your point across, establish brand trust, and convince them to stay longer. If your content doesn't resonate with them immediately, or if it's hard for them to purchase a product or contact you, they will leave.

Do not use pre-designed templates if you want users to remember you. Your business needs to be unique, different from competitors, and custom-tailored to your exact goals and strategy. Customization is key.

You'll also want to consider how to build in backend functionality to your website. Frequently in the form of 'plugins', these off-the-shelf applications facilitate a number of things, including SEO, a web store, contact forms, maps, etc.

As you can tell, there are a lot of considerations to evaluate before selecting a hosting provider, choosing a platform, and ultimately building your website. If you don't have experience with designing and maintaining websites, you may want to consider working with a web designer to make sure your website helps to grow your business in an effective way.

I provided some basic information in terms of graphic and website design, but there are other branding pieces that can be combined with the above, such as flyers, banners, brochures, and gift cards. And not just that—branding also includes video, advertising, and images. Depending on your brand strategy and where your target market hangs out, you will know if you need to invest in some of these things. But the most important thing to remember is all of your designs should be based on your brand strategy. **Brand strategy is the foundation for everything.**

14 How to Translate Strategy into Visuals

Now that you have your brand strategy, you're ready to translate the words into visuals, which is what your clients will be attracted to. This should be an easy process since we already know what your brand is, how it needs to sound to others, what kind of voice it should have, who your target is, and what your brand goal is. You might need to hire a professional designer who can help you with his or her knowledge of using the right design programs.

To translate your strategy into visuals, you need to start from the brand attributes that you previously defined. In Chapter 4: Brand Attributes, we talked about the attributes that describe your culture, customers, voice, and emotions/feelings. Your attributes are the base for your designs.

If one of your words to describe your brand's culture is "fun," your visuals need to look "fun." What does that mean? Can you name three things that feel fun when you look at them? This is a brainstorming process, and your designer should be able to help you come up with ideas and examples. What comes to my mind as fun is a birthday party, balloons, amusement park, playing games with friends, etc. Fun is something colorful, something busy, something interesting. To capture this element of fun in your visual identity, your designs could be multicolored, and you could use creative fonts and interesting images that capture attention.

After you describe your culture through visuals, you would move to the next brand attribute, which is your customer. Let's say that your customer is "educated." What does educated look like to you, and what images remind you of that word? You could include photos of schools, books, and glasses on your website, and your target will resonate with them.

How about your brand voice? Your brand voice is how you sound to others, and it will actually translate into your visuals the most. If your voice is "friendly," you will need to include images that demonstrate friendliness to your target since that is the way your brand speaks to them. What would be friendly? Maybe photos of two people meeting for a coffee or going to happy hours, a family during lunch, or people smiling. Think about how bigger brands demonstrate their brand voices through their visuals. Apple sounds innovative because their branding looks innovative, it sounds modern because their visuals look modern, and it sounds knowledgeable because their designs look cutting-edge.

The next brand attribute is emotions. If you wanted potential buyers to feel relaxed, how would you make them feel relaxed through your visuals? Think about how spas make their customers feel relaxed: they use soft colors, they include photos of people who are resting, and their language is serene and peaceful. You can refer to Chapter 12: Psychology as Universal Communication for more ideas on how to use colors, shapes, and placements to evoke specific emotions from your audience.

Once you combine all of these, you can easily translate your brand strategy into visuals. This is a process that includes some brainstorming and research, and your visuals can be created through a **mood board** (not a brand board, but mood board). A mood board is a board that visually represents all of your brand attributes. A mood board can contain different fonts, images, and colors, and you can think of it as a collage that looks and sounds just like your brand. When you look at that board, it needs to sound like those few words you chose for your brand. Have you ever made a vision board before? Your mood board is very similar to a vision board, except it's focused on your brand and brand attributes.

My examples above were: f*un, educated, friendly,* and r*elaxed.* You don't have to show all the attributes in one piece of the design. You can use fun colors for the concept of *fun,* photos with people working on their laptops for the concept of *educated,* a lot of shapes that are connected and remind you of friendship for the concept of *friendly,* and a layout with a lot of white space that would look peaceful for the concept of *relaxed.*

From here, you would focus on your target. What do *they* want to see? Let's say that your ideal client is 38 years old. You would want to make sure all your friendly images include people who are about that age. If your ideal client is married, it would be a good idea to feature families as much as you can, but if he/she is single you would use only photos with friends in them. Your target might like to read books, and if that's the case, why not use the word "reading" in your content? If she likes meditation, why not use curvy lines in your designs that helps her feel like she is relaxed and in good hands?

There are a lot of different things to consider before going into visuals, but a lot of business owners make the mistake of skipping over the brand strategy entirely. They choose a color *they* like, fonts *they* like, and images that resonate with *them*, and they start branding their company with these things, and they completely forget that visuals are here to attract their potential clients, not them.

After you make a mood board from your brand attributes, you can do a quick exercise of mind mapping too. To start the mind mapping process, put the name of your company in the center of a piece of paper. Then, surround that word (the name of your company) with 6–10 words that are close to it. Consider the specialty, services, nature of your business, brand voice, and maybe location—whatever comes to mind first. These words need to be your first thoughts, so don't spend too much time on it.

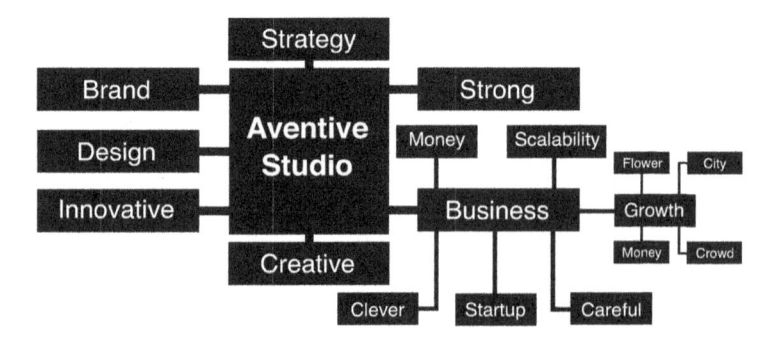

Aventive Studio: Mind Mapping Example

Then you can expand on each word. For example, on the mind map for my branding company I would have *Aventive Studio*, and then my first few words around that would be *brand, business, design, strategy, creative, strong,* and *innovative*. Next, I would expand and add more words around each one. For example, around *business* I would write *startup, growth, scalability, careful, money,* and *clever*. Then I would expand upon each of these words and try to come up with objects that I can visually use. The word *growth* would have words around it such as *flower, city, money,* or *crowd*—everything that is growing that reminds me of "a lot" or "more and more." I could use a video of a growing flower for my website, for example, and that would be a way to translate from my strategy into visuals. I provided just a few examples here, but a designer would put more thought and research into this, and they would probably start with a logo design first, so perhaps the logo would include a flower to symbolize growth.

Feel free to do your own mind mapping. Just take a pen and paper and dive deep into your business, your brand attributes, your ideal client, and your brand goals. Simply write as many things as you can, and then expand on them.

Once you have the mood board and mind mapping completed, you can start working on your logo design, business cards, website, and other design elements that are necessary to help you grow your business. You or a designer you hire would reference your brand strategy document the whole time while working on your designs. Match your designs to your content strategy, color meanings, or goals—whatever pieces will help you ensure that your visual branding matches your brand strategy and helps you scale your business.

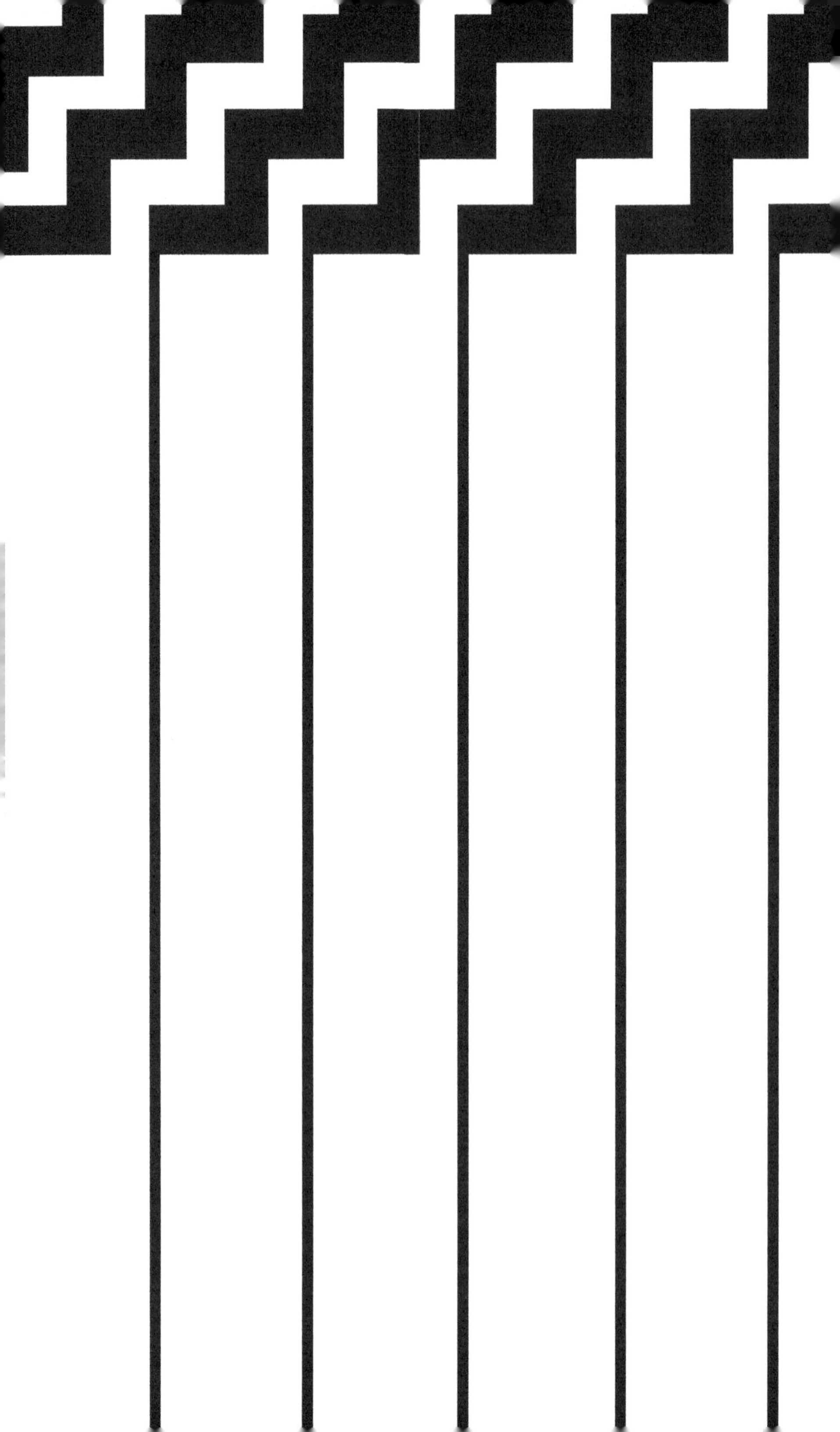

15 Strategic Elements and Execution

So, what's next? Where do you go from here? Assuming *BrandFix* has helped you clarify your goals, identify your 'why,' and determine what your brand actually is (and what it should and could be), you will be able to develop a brand strategy that guides all of your marketing and advertising efforts. Your brand strategy is the foundation of a successful business. I truly believe that every business owner can have a scalable business, but only if you're smart about what steps to take inside the company—basically following your brand strategy when it comes to what, why, how, and when everything needs to be done. Once you have a road map, you will know where to go and how to get there.

Since every business is different, it will be up to you or your marketing team (if you have one) to determine and prioritize your next steps. Your brand strategy will provide direct input to graphic designers, web designers and developers, marketing and advertising specialists, social media marketers, copywriters and content developers, promotion specialists, sales professionals, and any other professional that provides a service relevant to your brand or target audience.

We covered self-reflective brand discovery, identifying your entity's differentiation through brand positioning (differences between you and other businesses), characterizing your brand by its brand attributes and brand voice, understanding your target audience by their user profiles, establishing your approach to content generation through content strategy, and aligning your branding goals with your internal business goals. This completes your strategic foundation. Then, we expanded to online and offline businesses, business-to-business and business-to-consumer brands, how to brand products, what to do with services, and we even covered some external branding topics such as visuals—logo design, stationery, brand boards, and websites.

Any time you feel stuck, or when you're not sure what to do next with your branding, review the sections that cover the specific topic with which you're struggling. Reread chapters in order to learn them better. Branding is an ongoing process, and you will likely need to return to the book several times as your brand and your audience both grow.

However, my first suggestion would be to go straight back to Chapter 5 (Target Profiles) and revisit who your target is, what their problems are, how you can solve those problems, and where you can find these potential buyers. If you take away only one concept from this book, I want it to be this: You need to design your brand exclusively for your target audience. If you ever find yourself confused around branding, or if you wonder if something in your content is "off-brand," return to that concept and double-check that you're keeping your target in mind with every blog post, every picture, and every color selection that you make.

To tie up all the things that we've covered in this book, we will finish with a tangible and executable concept that I call **strategic elements.**

Strategic elements are the elements that come after the brand strategy and visuals. These include the use of your logo, website, business cards, and flyers paired with a plan on how to promote your business and attract your ideal client. We briefly mentioned these elements in previous chapters. If you know that Rachel is hanging out in a bar around the corner, you would need to create flyers and leave them in that bar so she can see them and find out that your business exists. So in this case, your flyer would be the strategic element for how to get in front of Rachel.

Everything that is under the umbrella of "marketing" counts as a strategic element. This includes your content marketing, your blogs, books and e-books, videos, podcasts, and everything educational and valuable that you create. You will use your brand voice every time you write an article. You will use your brand attributes every time you develop a new video that you can promote in order to reach your potential buyers. You will also use your content strategy in all of the above.

Then, social media... are you afraid of it? You have probably heard that social media can be good for your business, and maybe you already use it, but it does take time, and it's sometimes hard to develop ideas and figure out what to post in terms of images and text that people would like. Now that you have a brand strategy and content strategy in hand, you know exactly who your target is, and you can simply speak to them like they're in the same room as you. Using the social channels where your target hangs out, you can give them advice, educate them using your brand voice, post using the right brand colors that psychologically describe what your brand stands for, and be consistent with your visuals (after you develop the brand board) so they remember your company.

You would also use your competitor analysis and brand positioning in order to stand out from your competitors when on social media. Social media is a saturated place, and you need to rely on your brand strategy to make sure that your content is different, memorable, and better than your competition. You can also consider using paid social media posts and ads. Depending on your business, you will need to determine whether this is a good idea or not. Also worth considering is whether you are targeting a cold or warm audience. A **cold audience** is not specifically and actively looking for what you offer, but they might be interested in purchasing after seeing your product. A **warm audience** is already ready to purchase, they are looking for a product or services you offer, and they are researching to decide if they should select your company or your competitors'.

For example, with my branding company, I know that in order to contact me, people need a brand strategy, a logo design, or a website. They need to actively search for the solution of their problem. An ad on a site would not make them suddenly decide that they need a logo. On the other hand, when people work from home, feel lonely, are on social media, and see an ad about a coworking space, they click on it because they are curious to learn more. Most of them are not actively looking for a coworking space until they see the ad and think

"Huh. Maybe I should try that out." So it depends on the nature of your business and what you think would work for you and your target. Is your target actively looking for a solution of their problem? Or they are not aware that they have a problem just yet? Don't be afraid to test both approaches to see which is more effective.

You can still use offline advertising and promoting to reach new customers—not everything has to be online, especially if you're targeting local customers in your area. Networking events are amazing in terms of meeting new people, building relationships, and collaborating with referral partners. There are individuals who can help you grow your business as well. If you meet a videographer who helps you create an amazing promotional video, and you make money from it because a new client contacted you after seeing the video on a Facebook ad, that sale was the result of both the networking event you attended and your online advertising. We still have billboards in all cities and towns, and we still have posters, newspapers, local magazines, radio, and TV. These options can be a little expensive, and you don't receive the same granular level of data on how many people saw your ad and responded, in contrast to online marketing and advertising where you can see how many people clicked on your website. But depending on your company and target, offline advertising might be worth it. Go back to your strategy, and then go where your target is.

You can also consider ordering branded promotional material. This "swag" is more for brand awareness than for promotion. You can make stickers, pens, or mouse pads—there are so many different product options. When considering promotional products, it's important to realize that swag will likely not bring you new business immediately. If you have already talked to someone, but they lost your business card and don't remember the name of your company, and they suddenly remember they have a pen that they took from your office, swag can help. It can happen that they contact you because of the swag, but they will most likely contact you because they already interacted with you and know who you are and what your offerings are.

When considering which strategic elements to employ for your brand, look at all the notes and materials you have created while reading this book. You already know your brand attributes, your target, and how to communicate your brand both visually and through content. **You have everything you need to get out there, take action, and use your shiny new brand to scale your business and reach new customers.**

Entrepreneurship is not for the faint of heart. For all the risks you're taking, and for all the heart and money that you have poured into making your business a success, it's worth spending time to learn how to communicate your work through a strong brand.

You can build a brand that reflects your business exquisitely. You can have such engaging content and visuals that your target audience says, "*Where* has this company been all of my life, and how can I sign up?" All of that is available to you, and it all starts with developing your brand strategy. Whatever you decide to do with your business, your brand strategy is the foundation, and if you follow the steps I outlined in this book, you will be well on your way to a thriving and successful brand that scales your business. Now just take the action and you will see the results!

Want More Branding Support?

Here is your Branding Checklist which includes everything a business needs in order to have a successful brand. If you have any questions, comments, or feedback, or if you simply need help with developing your brand strategy or designs, feel free to reach out to Kady Sandel at hello@AventiveStudio.com.

BRANDING CHECKLIST

Internal Branding

- ☐ **Brand Discovery and Audit**
    - Mission
    - Vision
    - Values
- ☐ **Brand Positioning and Messaging**
    - Competitor analysis
    - Product / Service differentiation
    - Positioning statement
- ☐ **Brand Attributes**
    - Culture
    - Emotion
    - Impact
- ☐ **Brand Voice**
- ☐ **Target Market**
    - Customer research
    - Target profiles

- ☐ **Content Strategy**
  - Goals
  - Target
- ☐ **Business Goal Alignment**

External Branding

- ☐ **Brand Identity**
  - Logo Design
  - Mood Board
  - Brand Board
    - Logo variations
    - Color hex codes
    - Typography
    - Styled imagery
  - Brand Guideline
    - Placement & how to use brand assets
- ☐ **Corporate Stationery**
  - Business cards
  - Envelopes
  - Letterhead
- ☐ **Marketing Collateral**
  - Flyers, brochure, posters...
- ☐ **Website Design & Development**
  - Platform selection
    - Domain and hosting
  - Layout and styles
  - Website goals
- ☐ **SEO**
  - Platform selection
  - Website setup (correct layout)
  - Relevant content (headers, text and blog)
  - Using the right keywords

- Backlinks
- [ ] **Digital Marketing and Advertising**
- [ ] **Copywriting**
  - Content marketing/resources and blog
  - Email marketing
- [ ] **Photography & Video**
- [ ] **Social Media**
  - Scheduling and management tools
    - Facebook
    - Instagram
    - Twitter
    - Google+ (for business)
- [ ] **Business Pages**
  - Google My Business Page
  - Yelp
- [ ] **Web Tools (partial list—must-haves only)**
  - Google Analytics
  - Google Search Console
  - Email hosting and distribution tools
- [ ] **Advertising**
  - Facebook ads
  - Google ads
  - Retargeting, PPC
- [ ] **Promotional material & printing (swag)**
  - Pens, mouse pads, notepads, etc.
- [ ] **Outreach**
  - News/PR
  - Sponsorships/civic involvement/memberships
  - Networking
  - Testimonials
  - Reviews (establishing trust)

About the Author

Kady Sandel is the CEO, Creative Director, and Brand Strategist of Aventive Studio. Kady moved from her home at age 15 to launch a career in graphic design, and she has designed logos, websites, and visual identities for a wide range of business clients. In her time as a designer, she developed a passion for helping businesses scale through creating memorable and strategic brands.

An entrepreneur at heart, Kady is also the founder of MELD Coworking in Austin, Texas. She was named 2018 Entrepreneur of the Year by the Austin Business Owners Networking Group, and she speaks to audiences about effective branding and networking strategies. She loves cats to a fault and can usually be found drinking coffee with copious amounts of creamer.

Connect with Kady

Here are a few ways to stay connected with Kady Sandel:

- Visit www.AventiveStudio.com to contact Kady, book a brand strategy consultation, sign up for e-mail updates, and see examples of her studio's services and design work.
- Connect with @AventiveStudio on Facebook or Instagram.
- If you enjoyed this book, consider leaving a review on Amazon. This small action will help more busy entrepreneurs discover BrandFix, learn about branding, and scale their businesses through brand strategy

Made in United States
North Haven, CT
22 September 2022